The
Cabin

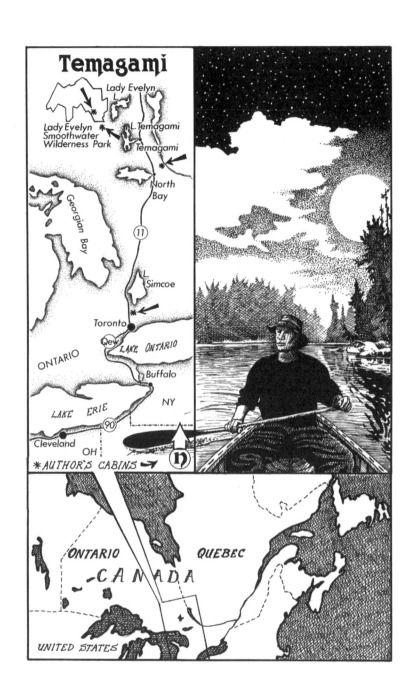

The
Cabin

A Search for Personal Sanctuary

Hap Wilson

NATURAL HERITAGE BOOKS
TORONTO

Published by Natural Heritage / Natural History Inc.
P.O. Box 95, Station O, Toronto, Ontario M4A 2M8
www.naturalheritagebooks.com

Library and Archives Canada Cataloguing in Publication

Wilson, Hap, 1951-
The cabin : a search for personal sanctuary / Hap Wilson.

ISBN 1-897045-05-0

1. Wilson, Hap, 1951-. 2. Outdoor life—Ontario—Temagami Region.
3. Temagami Region (Ont.)—Biography. I. Title.

FC3099.T425Z49 2005   971.3'147   C2005-906277-0

All illustrations in this book, including the cover illustrations, are by the author.
Cover and text design by Neil Thorne
Edited by Jane Gibson
Printed and bound in Canada by Hignell Book Printing of Winnipeg

Natural Heritage / Natural History Inc. acknowledges the financial support of the Canada Council for the Arts and the Ontario Arts Council for our publishing program. We acknowledge the support of the Government of Ontario through the Ontario Media Development Corporation's Ontario Book Initiative. We also acknowledge the financial support of the Government of Canada through the Book Publishing Industry Development Program (BPIDP) and the Association for the Export of Canadian Books.

To the Lathrops—Dick, Dan & Jim—
whose altruistic and gracious brotherhood
allowed me to find my own freedom.

Contents

Preamble: Transformation   *i*

One: The Trout Streams   1

Two: The Rapidan Club   11

Three: The Pine Tree   21

Four: Hyde's Cabin and The Dirty Dozen Club   33

Five: Life Underground   41

Six: Cabin Falls   49

Seven: Winter on Diamond Lake   67

Eight: Nitchee Keewense   75

Nine: Snake Creek Homestead   89

Ten: Paradise Under Siege   101

Eleven: Transcendence   113

Twelve: Civil Disobedience   123

Thirteen: Conflagration   131

Fourteen: King of Sladen Township   139

Fifteen: Paradise Below Zero   147

Afterword   *169*

About the Author   *173*

Books by Hap Wilson   *175*

"Every river that flows is good, and has something worthy to be loved. But those that we love most are always the ones that we have known best."
Henry Van Dyke—Little Rivers, 1895

Preamble: Transformation

Nenebuc, the trickster, had his bow and arrow with him, and as he went along he saw a great snake. He shot his arrow, killed the snake, and turned it into a long, rocky ridge to which he named ish-pud-in-ong.[1] He soon came to shonj-a-waw-gaming,[2] a large lake with a beautiful sandy shore, where he saw several Mishipeshu—the giant lynx bathing in the water. Nenebuc couldn't shoot them with his arrow as they were too far away, nor was there any place where he could hide himself until they came to sun themselves by the beach, when they felt too cold in the water. Finally, Nenebuc had a plan. He took some birch bark from a rotten stump, rolled it into a hollow cylinder, and placed it, like a wigwam, near the shore. He then climbed inside and made a little hole in the bark through which to shoot and kill the Mishipeshu.

When the Mishipeshu saw the thing on the beach, they grew curious to find out what this strange thing was that had not been there the day before. So, they sent a big snake to twist around it and try to upset it, but the snake did not succeed in doing this because Nenebuc stood too firm. So, the Mishipeshu came ashore upon the white sand beach and Nenebuc shot one of them with his arrow—the wife of the lion chief. He did not kill her, but wounded her badly in the side, and the flint arrow-point stayed in the wound. The she-lion was very badly wounded and went back to a hole which led to a cave[3] in a big rock where she lived with her family. Nenebuc was sorry that he had not killed the Mishipeshu queen.

The following morning, as he walked along the shore, Nenebuc heard someone singing and shaking a rattle. He stood there wondering and waiting, and soon he saw an old woman making the song. So he went across to see her, and when they met, he asked her, "What are you doing?" "I'm a doctor," she answered. "The Mishipeshu queen has been shot by Nenebuc and I am going to cure her." She didn't know that it was Nenebuc to whom she was talking, for she was too old. Nenebuc told her, "Let me hear you singing. Is that what you are going to do to

---

1 Ishpatina (Ishpudinong) Ridge is the highest point in Ontario, situated at the west boundary of Lady Evelyn-Smoothwater Wilderness Park.

2 Known today as Smoothwater Lake, it is renowned for its Caribbean-like beach, clear water and breathtaking landscape.

3 This cave is purported to be on a rocky bluff on the west shore of Smoothwater Lake. I have actually tried to locate this cave but to no avail.

cure her?" "Yes, I will sing and then pull out that arrow." The Mishipeshu had sent for her at the foot of the lake to cure the queen. Nenebuc picked up a club and killed her, saying, "You are no macki-ki-winini'kwe, [medicine-person woman] at all." Then he discovered that she was no person at all either, but a big oma-kaki [large toad]. So, he skinned her and put on the skin. The skin had a hole in the groin, and as he had no needle to sew it up with, his scrotum hung out. This did not worry Nenebuc, for he thought, "It will be alright, unless they notice me too closely." So, he walked past the cave in which the Mishipeshu lived and kept singing and rattling for some time.

When the young cats heard him, they said, "There's the old medicine woman coming." They were very glad to think that their mother would be cured. So they opened the door in the rock and Nenebuc went in, and one of the daughters came to meet him and said, "Come in, old woman." They were very much pleased. Nenebuc said, "Don't shut the doors. Leave them open, as the queen needs plenty of fresh air!" Then, he said, "I'm hungry. I've had a long walk and I'm tired." Then they gave him a good meal first. While he was eating, he sat with open legs and the children cried out, "Look at the old woman with testicles hanging out!" But the older ones told them to be silent, as they thought some old women had testicles.

When he had finished eating, Nenebuc said, "Don't watch me. I'm going to pull out the arrow-point. You will hear her suffering and me singing, but don't look until you hear her stop suffering. Then she will be cured, and the arrow-point will be out. So, don't look, for I am going to cure her." Then he began rattling and singing, and as he did so, he shoved the arrow-point farther into the wound of the queen in order to kill her. When she yelled, her people thought that the hurt was caused in pulling the arrow out. At last, one of the little Mishipeshu children peeped and saw Nenebuc pushing the arrow farther in. He told his sister, "That's Nenebuc himself inside!" Then Nenebuc ran outside and the queen was dying. Nenebuc had difficulty escaping. He pulled off the toad skin and tried to climb up the steep rock.

Once the queen died, a giant stream poured out of the cave and the lake began rising. "That is going to flood the world and be the end," said Nenebuc. So, he cut trees and made an abin-desagan [a kind of raft]. So, he had his raft ready, and the end of the world came. He couldn't see any trees, water covered everything, and he made the flood. Nenebuc saw all kinds of animals swimming toward his raft and he took them on. "Come on, come on," he cried, "and stay here." Nenebuc wanted to save them, so that after the flood there would be all kinds of animals. The animals stayed on the raft with him for a long while. Some time after this he *made a rope of roots and tied it to the Beaver's tail, telling him to dive and to try to reach the land underneath. The Beaver couldn't reach the land at the bottom and he came up to the surface again.*

Seven days after this he allowed the Muskrat to try and bring the land from the bottom. Muskrat dove and they waited a long time, but he didn't come up. Upon diving, the muskrat doubled up and put his nose into the hair of his breast which enabled him to breathe by the bubbles clinging there. By doing this he could rest and dive still deeper. At last he used up all the air in his breast hair and could only grab a little piece of mud from the bottom. Then he started up to the surface of the water but drowned before he reached the raft. Nenebuc pulled the Muskrat in and saw that he was still holding the mud in his paw. Nenebuc said, "I am going to dry this. As soon as it is dry, you can all run around again and have this world." So he dried it, but not entirely, and that is the reason why some parts of the world are swampy and wet, while others are dry. So, the animals had the earth again and the world was made. And it was called, Tem-ee-ay-gaming.[4]

The poignant and whimsical Ojibwa account of recreation embraces the essential fabric of this book. Most of the story is magnetically ensconced within the undulating and primal folds of the Temagami wilderness. I was lured to and seduced by the landscape; soulful journeys that pacified the restlessness within and the provision of both sanctuary and peace of mind. Metaphorically, I suppose, this provocative tale of rebirth attempts to substantiate and reconceptualize my own wanderings as a purely abstract approach to life experiences and expectations. Much of what unfolded and inspired me, and continues to unfold, relates to direct experiences that were often non-objective, incidental, or evolutionary. Nenebuc had no idea that his actions, extreme as they were, would have such immense repercussions that, by sheer designlessness, actually evolved into some other nirvanic reality. Chaos leads to order. Sometimes, if desired.

In 1971, upon finishing high school I was offered a permanent illustrating job in Toronto. The salary was extravagant, the work purportedly monotonous; I declined the job as it would have interfered with a planned canoe trip organized for that summer. Irrational? Perhaps. The Zen of free-living was already an ineffable reality, and the buzz was all consuming. In my own mind there was no fixed definition of Nature, or Wilderness, and my sojourns by canoe and snowshoe were highlighted by a state of consciousness that allowed

---

4   Taken from F.G. Speck, "Myths and Folklore of the Timiskaming Algonquin and Temagami Ojibwa," Canada Department of Mines based on interviews with Benjamin Mackenzie of the Timiskaming band, 1913.

whatever to happen, *happen*. I was an incurable romantic and devout dreamer. Transformation came about insidiously through a series of revelations and events, mostly detached from, but reluctantly a part of a dysfunctional family dynamic. My father was an abusive workaholic and suffered an early stroke; three uncles succumbed soon after early retirement after having devoted their respective adult lives to callous employers. My parents, my whole family it seemed, were extremely driven by an intense need to succeed beyond their means. The patriarchs of my family were not particularly devoted fathers, in the spiritual sense, nor did they portray themselves as savoury role models; but they did nonetheless, provide the basic necessities required to raise a family according to the rules of good housekeeping, *à la* 1950s and '60s. There was something missing in this mantra. Something deeper, I thought, and I remained perplexed by their criticisms applied to my wilderness leanings away from the mainstream. I was admonished for not seeking what *they* espoused as a *real job,* one that implied a sense, at least, of honour, security and responsibility. Artists are inveterate prevaricators; I was told, lazy Bohemians, and worst of all—*poor.* My passion for the wilderness trail and total lack of respect for money consolidated my unorthodox persuasions. My canoe lodged somewhere along the shore without being swept away by the rising flood.

I rebelled. Adopting an unconventional lifestyle, I was free to make my own choices. Not all of them were wise ones but, in the least, I brandished a desire to stand true to my somewhat recalcitrant beliefs. My parents' narcissistic compulsions and languorous parental enthusiasm, acted like rust on the metal framework bonding our family together. Our home became an inveterate battleground and I slipped out the backdoor whenever possible, leaving the folks alone to duke it out. My older siblings evolved in their way, and I took to the woods. When the corrosion rotted out the pith of stability and the family home lost its stature as sanctuary, I was compelled to seek solace elsewhere. Oddly enough, against the obvious odds, I enjoyed a wonderful childhood that had little to do with my parents, and everything to do with a dogged tenacity to explore the natural world out my backdoor. And in retrospect, I can either blame or thank my maladjusted parents for my antediluvian obsessions that have prevailed into mid-life (I still do not have a real job). Without their incessant bickering, inducing me to sneak out of my bedroom window at age fourteen to sleep in a woodlot teepee, I would never have found paradise.

The Cabin was not written as an autobiography, as such, but a collection of stories that perceivably embraces a search for reason, first, sanctuary secondly.

It is hoped it won't be perceived as some vain attempt to flaunt or dictate a deviant approach to fitting in to societal mainstream unconsciousness, but to share with you—the neo-homesteader, the revolutionary Guevarist, the eco-warrior, the dreamer—a construct of my own meanderings as cabin-builder, wood-butcher, park ranger (with attitude) and usufractuary.

Henry David Thoreau built a cabin on the shores of Walden Pond. No permits. No taxes. No mortgage. It cost him little but the dividends were immense. However brief his stay in the woods had been, his labour was garnished with the satisfaction that he lived simply, cheaply and happily. Time. Labour. Both had little to do with the quality of the experience. Bodhidharma—a Buddhist Saint, travelling through China, met the Chinese Emperor. The Emperor asked him how much merit had he gained through his building of monasteries, the patronizing of translators and the praise of monks and nuns. "None," Bodhidharma[5] answered, "these are inferior deeds. These objects are mere shadows. The only true work of merit is wisdom, pure, perfect and mysterious, which is not to be won through material acts."

Is it not true then, that what one perceives, absorbs, and reflects upon, (ignoring the complications and tedium of time and labour), a pure task with associated risks—*the adventure*—is the springboard that elevates life to a blissful grandeur? Life should be so simple. Buddhists believe in Zen, particularly *Satori—the experience of direct enlightenment,* preparing the individual for a sudden, unexpected enlightenment that rises above desire and suffering—action rather than theory. If one were to cross-pollinate Daoist belief with the transcendent profanity of the "Beat Generation," we'd see Jack Kerouac and Allen Ginsberg yielding to the natural flow of the universe, smoking pot, while casually paddling a canoe down a wild river in northern Canada. If, at the time of my youth, I had any alliances with earthly-minded Philistinistic icons, I'd be following in the wake of Kerouac's canoe, or throwing knives with Indian wannabe, Grey Owl.[6]

Having spent a good deal of my adult life in a canoe, or strapped to snow-shoes, the distance attained trekking across this country could have vaulted me to the moon and back. But this is not what defines my life or the story herein, nor is the adventure simply a collection of personal deeds to brandish with pretension; it is the pure *mystery* of the challenge itself. The unknowing

---

5 Story related by Joseph Campbell, one of America's greatest modern-day philosophers.

6 Famous Canadian/English author who portrayed himself as an Indian and learned his trade as trapper and outdoorsman while paddling in Temagami in the early 1900s.

elements provoke deep emotions while fate is held ransom for knowledge. *This* is what stratifies my own selfness on the edge of modern reason.

Fortunately, much of what I have written has been extracted from volumes of field notes, diaries and journals I kept since I was a teenager. And although my memory serves me well, for certain things, the journals were indispensable for their simplicity, honesty and purity, and for the illustrations which I have transferred from pencil to pen and ink. So, in essence, aside from being presented as an historiographical chronology, it is very much an adventure story, perhaps a manual for those seeking the Zen of free-living without the impedimenta of societal overburdens. It is a curious attempt at mingling the absurd with the natural and an inevitable compulsion for freedom.

Hap Wilson, 2005

One: The Trout Streams

Thus it has lain since the world was young,
enveloped in a mystery beyond understanding,
and immersed in silence, absolute, unbroken,
and all-embracing…
Grey Owl, 1932

The broad back of the Precambrian Shield sweeps across Canada. From the eastern ramparts of the inimical Labrador coast, westward, circling Hudson Bay, pushing deep into the barren lands, this ancient lithosphere penetrates deep into the arctic islands. Time's weary mantle lays bare the carapace of Mother Earth—the world's oldest rock—consolidated of Archaean basalt, shifted by graben faulting, worn down through the millennia, the majesty of mountains past, now modest and recumbent. Along its central orientation, below James Bay, there is a marked rise in elevation—a broken, low plateau that sits a thousand feet above the surrounding landscape. At its apex, Ish-pud-inong Ridge overshadows the tapestry of lakes, fens and streams below. It is the highest mountain for eight hundred kilometres (five hundred miles) to the east and south, and sixteen hundred kilometres (a thousand miles) to the west and north. Clouds seem to hesitate momentarily at its loftiness, then drift lazily northeast, pushed by the prevailing southwesterlies.

A day's paddle by canoe to the north lay Smoothwater Lake. According to local Ojibwa mythology, *Nenebuc*—the impenitent trickster slew the great lynx here, causing a world flood. Fortunately for *Nenebuc*, the deluge would have quickly dissipated and channelled off into *shonj-a-waw-ga-maw, na-may,* and *ma-ja-may-gos* river headwater outlets, for there is no other place higher in this part of the world, and from here all water makes the long journey to the ocean.

It is from the long, white sand beach on the east shore of Smoothwater Lake where we begin our journey down the Trout Streams—*ma-ja-may-gos-sibi.* The events that shaped the land, the people who camped here since the exodus of the great ice sheets, the vestiges of unprovoked documentation, are alive and memorialized in myth, magic and majesty ensconced within the primal landscape, a reality as pure and lucid now as it was thousands of years ago. And if I were to tell you that this journey through Temagaming—as the ancients called Temagami—along the Trout Streams, we would arrive at a place that in every conceivable imagining was the most beautiful place on this earth, *would you believe me if you hadn't seen it for yourself?* Probably not.

I was prepared for this, and that is why we brought along the canoe. It's an old wood and canvas canoe, a "Peterborough" in fact, a classic design, a prospector. This canoe is a fine lady of the river, resplendent in style and grace, yet practical and fearless when the need arises. Don't pay heed to the amberoid patches on her bottom, or the tin can lids pushed up between the ribs to shore the broken planking—she's old but endowed with capable aplomb. And the need for consummate skill will arise when we hit the rapids, two days hence, beyond the junction of the two river branches. In all it is a three-day canoe trip to where we are going. *And where might that be you ask?* To Paradise I say, where The Cabin sits at the precipice of a magnificent cascade, and where the pines sway to the music of the falls. Time is of the least concern here because all cares and appointments are quickly forgotten as you revel in the now, consumed by the flood of sensual responses. And once there, we can sit with our backs to the wood stove and our bellies to the plank table and sip our whisky from tin cups, and exchange revelations about the trip down the river.

A sense of urgency is galvanized by your curiosity and we push off into the translucent waters, heading south to the headwaters of the river. The lake does not yield easily to its namesake and we push steadily against heavy waves until we reach the bay where the portage is located. The trail is well worn, more from the trampling of moose than of men. We shoulder our packs and walk across, then go back again for the canoe and our fishing rods. Blackflies are thick now as the temperature rises and our sweaty bodies send out the message that breakfast is now being served. *This is hell, not paradise,* you remark as you flail your arms madly at the biting hordes, making them even more intent on stripping a man's dignity and self-composure. *You'll get used to them,* I lie. The canoe is reloaded. It's a short paddle across Apex Lake. Beaver grass and cattails line the shore, backed by stunted black spruce and tamarack just starting to bud. The world tips off in all directions. Another portage, longer this time, and we arrive at the headwater lake with the fitting name of Whitemud. You remark about the blackness of the pool below the rock shelf where we placed our packs. Those are speckled trout, brookies if you like, thicker than sardines in a can. We catch a half-dozen one-pounders for our lunch, gutting them quickly and grilling them over an open fire. Nothing tastes better.

This stretch of the Trout Streams has been known to break a man's spirit just by the sheer nastiness of it. The Anishnabek referred to it as *Toong-dee-ay*, meaning "asshole pointing backwards." Six miles of cedar swamp, flies and deadfalls, the river is no more than half-a-canoe width and plagued with sunken logs, gravel shallows and beaver dams. *The Ojibwa named it appropriately*, you think, as you grab the gunnels of the canoe and raise your backside to a low crouch, and try to jerk the boat off another submerged cedar, all the while ducking below the alder, festooned with spider webs and their trappings. You curse again and I explain that *Paradise does not come without a challenge.*

The sky is of empyrean blue, unflecked by even a trace of cumulus, and the smell of balsam and cedar so thick as to saturate each inhale with a full-bodied elixir. We press on. For the most part, the paddling is unobstructed and the early spring water levels are forgiving, allowing clearance over most of the deterrents. We stop to watch a cow moose and her newborn calf amble through the thicket of willow at the shore's edge; she watches with guarded eye, ears flicking and nostrils flared, urging her young charge to follow her into the hummocks beyond our line of vision.

At the end of the portage around the long rapid, where the Trout Stream spills off a terrace of bedrock, just before the junction of the Florence River, we have a few moments to cast our bait into the foamy pools. Within minutes, we have quite enough fish for a generous supper. Gulls circle, waiting to descend upon the pile of entrails left on a flat boulder beside our canoe. By now you've forgotten about the blackflies, or anything else for that matter, anything beyond the anticipation of what lies ahead around the next bend in the river, and what lure to use to catch the next trout.

Shkim-ska-jeeshing, or lake-that-bends-in-the-middle, known these days as Florence Lake, is the largest body of water feeding the Trout Streams by way of a short, broad and shallow river. It is flanked by huge white pines and home to at least one nest of fish hawk or osprey, set upon the apogee of a chicot (dead, standing timber), just up from the junction. I suggest we stop here for a pipe and reflect on the difference in the clarity of the water—the Florence River having a phthalo-green transparency, while the Trout Stream's organic hue was that of iron oxide—a sepia brown concoction that obscures the depths and conceals the most nuisance of rocks that lie just under the surface. We float gently in the current watching the eelgrass below the canoe undulate like prairie wheat in the wind. *You want to know more about Florence Lake.*

This is a place of such quiet reserve as to beguile the senses. The Temeaugama anishnabe gave it its name after a fold of land that buckles back to form a broad bend in the centre of the lake, the spit of land thus separating the main body of water is but a mere ten paces across, making for an easy lift over. The isthmus also calms the lake on a windy day so that the waves never exceed one's ability to safely navigate a canoe from one end of the lake to the other—a distance of about ten kilometres (six miles). It is surrounded by hills. To the west lies a ridge of such distinction and height that the sun sets by early afternoon behind it; to the east rises a shield of vertical rock that captures and reflects the sanguine blush of evening light. This conflagration of colour is soft and inconspicuous at first, rising in a rubicund crescendo as the sun tips over the west horizon. The lake water is a lucid ultramarine that enables the eye to see submerged objects to a depth of more than ten fathoms. Cool to the taste, never tepid as summer water often is, this lake is springfed. The canoe seems not to float at all on Florence but to be suspended in aqueous weightlessness, elevated by the magic that dwells in such places of remarkable beauty. Ancient pines crowd the shoreway, each tree demonstrative of the power of the prevailing southwest wind, branches tipped and reaching outstretched, upward with fingers extended. There is a beach running the breadth of a small bay guarded by a prominent granite buttress, behind which sits a long, sloped, bedrock terrace where a large canoe party could easily pitch half a dozen canvas tents. From the vantage of the beach, on a still day, if you viewed the vault of rock framing the backside of the campsite, the totem reflections would reveal the face of *mish-a-pishu,* the great underwater lynx. The residing totems—the kingfisher and the beaver— belong to the *kamino-kama,* standing solidly family, and *Misa-bi,* giant man family. Hunting grounds that takes three days to paddle across, cover an area of over 2,590 square kilometres (1,000 square miles) in all. If you looked carefully, perhaps walked along the beach at the narrows, or noticed a large tipped-up rock on a point north of the campsite, you would see fragments of their history, in dolmen stones, quartz-tooling fragments, serpent formations and encampments long since abandoned.

With the tobacco in our pipes now spent, we resume our paddling. Sedge and alder crowd the shores, half-submerged in the spring wash. It's silent except for the *wheedle-wheedle-dees* of the red-winged blackbirds flitting about noisily amongst the cattails. The river widens into a small lake and then constricts as we round a bend, turning us to face a granite monolith that suddenly bulls its way into the landscape. You rest your paddle on the gunnels as you take it all in. It looks as if the river ends here, at the foot of this escarpment, but it pauses only briefly; we gaze up at the steepness, eyes naturally following the line of cliffs that eventually fades and draws back into the forest. The scene tugs at your visual senses like a windlass until you are all consumed by the immensity of it, and you can do nothing until the spell is broken. The haunting warble of the hermit thrush from deep within the wood does nothing to interrupt the enchantment but only adds to the evening magic.

Our tent is pitched in the lengthening shadows, beneath tall pines, up on a bedrock knoll high above the river. The temperature dips quickly once the sun touches the tops of the trees across from our campsite—a godsend really, because now it is too cool for blackflies, even for mosquitoes. We sit quietly by the crackling fire, eating our trout while the smoke from the fire settles lazily over the flank of the river, mixing congenially with the rising mist. A chorale of spring peepers fills the air with woodland melody—the harmonious voice of creation. You are tired and it feels great. Sleep comes swiftly.

The sound of a raven wakes you; you scramble for your damp clothing and stick your head out of the tent and see that breakfast is already waiting for you by the fire. The canoe is quickly loaded and we slip away from shore, noiselessly so as not to disturb the morning quiescence. The river pinches through a cleft of grey granite forcing the current to pick up noticeably. You shift uneasily in your seat as the sound of rapids ahead fills the air with uncertain calamity. I explain that these are not difficult rapids, not big enough to warrant undue apprehension. It is good to be fearful though as fear sharpens the wit. You do well for your first descent and I see by the gleam in your eye that you can't wait for the next one. It will be a while now before the sound of a rapid is heard because we have reached the meanders where the rushes and meadow grass define the river in serpentine channels. The river coils back upon itself repeatedly in tight arcs, sometimes passing near the same gnarled tamarack three times before leaving it behind. We occasionally get out of the canoe to lower the boat over a beaver dam; the stretch is comforting to cramped leg muscles. We paddle for an hour—a distance of about five kilometres (three miles), yet, as the raven flies we have actually progressed a little more than one—the Trout Stream tricks us into thinking we've travelled a great distance. Swaths of reeds are pushed aside

by wading moose as they stroll with no particular urgency or directive except by their insatiable appetite.

We reach the confluence of the two branches, conjoining spirit and rhythm with verdant forest, deep, tangled and impenetrable. Quickly the river flows, and with a conservation of paddle strokes the canoe is manoeuvered into the dark "V" that pronounces the head of the rapids. We pass by the obvious trailhead—the portage circumventing the rapid—and commit ourselves to the run. You are about to say something but prudence keeps you silent lest any interruption breaks the concentration. Within seconds, the canoe is hurled downward, past sharp-edged boulders, any one of which might rip into the hull with unforgiving savagery; but moments later there is a pause as the canoe rests in the blackwater pool, floating victoriously in the deep eddy below the chute.

But this is just the beginning of many whitewater runs, and, after the initial unease you experienced during the first couple of runs, you relax into the adventure in a state of euphoria and anticipation. There are twelve rapids and falls on the way to The Cabin, some of them are run while others are lined down or portaged around; at the terminus of each we pull our rods and cast into the bottom pools. We catch most for the sport of it, releasing these precious gems back into their watery world, keeping only four trout for our dinner.

We reach our second campsite just as the sun begins its descent behind the crest of a high hill, a ridge where the pines cut into the pastel afternoon like an inverted saw blade. As you walk along the portage, you steal glimpses of a waterfall as it swirls around Precambrian granite, through fissures and over ledges, the tempo reaching a crescendo as we finish at a low platform of bedrock that faces the cascading river. Canoeists know this place as Shangri-La—aptly named as you assume there is no place more endearing than this one; but your weariness tells you that anywhere is the best spot to end the day. The sound is deafening and you soon realize that conversation is futile. Words seem almost trite and disrespectful. The night will be cool and clear and we will sleep under the stars, and all you can think about is the bear that left his mark along the portage trail upriver. To the east lies Dry Lake Ridge, basking in brassy magnificence as the alpenglow melts away to evening dusk. The Land of Shadows prevails with surreal and absolute omnipotence. Mist rises above the chutes as the air chills; the aroma of bush coffee emanates from a blackened pot perched at the edge of the campfire; activity rotates around the fireplace like planets around the sun. This place has an aura of magic about it, an ancientness marked by its assemblage of tumbled boulders, caves, grottos and abrupt outcroppings of spruce-studded scarps—a Tolkien landscape that sets the stage for all manner of Ojibwa sprites and forest gnomes—the *maymaygwishiwok,* the *paueehnsujk, paguk,* the flying skeleton, and even the dreaded *Wendigo*! You elect to sleep nearest the fire, and, when morning comes, you admit to having slept so well that you did not hear the booming caterwaul of a barred owl that, for several hours, had settled into a perch overlooking the campsite.

In the morning we move quickly to the canoe that lies overturned at the end of the portage at the base of the falls, load our gear and shove off. Before you can shake the morning chill from stiff limbs, the river sweeps to the left and drops through a series of tight rapids, so steep that you cannot see the bottom. The canoe is steered towards a channel between rocks where the water piles up into haystacks and small hydraulics. This is not a difficult run, but still a rather testy balancing act for such a diminutive craft that the embrace of one rock may precipitate a nasty pirouette.

Within moments, having been hurled through swifts and rapids without a chance of catching our breath, Divide Lake suddenly opens up before us, pushing the hills back far enough so that we can at least feel the probing heat from the morning sun. We drift awhile. A cow moose feeds in the shallows near the central narrows. A pair of loons cruises by curiously, surveying both canoe and its occupants, approves, and then glides away in disinterest. It is lovely here. The prevailing breeze carries us to the end of the lake where the river splits into two channels. We avoid the north channel; by the sound of it, there is an attitude of defiance as the river crashes through the broken rock. We steer for the south channel—a friendlier persuasion than its alter ego—still alive with boulders that seem to drift menacingly towards the approaching canoe. We make it down without incident and coast up to the portage that skirts a picturesque chute and rapids—a rather portentous falls defined by smoothly carved potholes and Moorish rock tectonics.

At the end of the portage, as you bargain for good footing amongst the scrabble of boulders, you notice a pair of merganser ducks sunning themselves on a flat rock by the river edge. At our presence, they slide off their perch into the current and scull off downstream. This is the final stretch before reaching our destination. The hills are steep here, topped by ancient red and white pine, braced along the slopes by a haphazard blend of hardwoods, spruce and cedar. Soon enough the river tips off out of view indicating a steep drop ahead. The low rumble of the falls grows slowly from inside your body; you feel it first rather than accept the notion that there is any sound at all that may indicate its presence until you are right at its precipice. We ease the canoe to river right and unload the packs up on shore. The boat is pulled up and I announce that you need only take your personal duffle over the portage. And you quickly discern that there is hardly a trail anyway—more like a scramble over and around boulders—no easy walk with a load on your back. The pines open up to a tilt of grey bedrock that runs from the rapids back to a thirty-metre (almost a hundred feet) canyon; set at the edge of the river is a small, unobtrusive log cabin overlooking the chasm of the falls. The scene is unlike anything else you've ever experienced except, perhaps in fairy book tales and fictional adventure novels. You put your pack down to gain a better perspective. Upstream you see where the river braids around vaults of rock—an archipelago of pine-topped islands—spilling its charge into multi-levelled bathing pools, continuing past The Cabin where it pauses briefly before being hurled over a ten-metre (eleven-yard) ledge. The ledge spans the width of the falls in chaotic and deeply carved fissures and tiered stratum so that there is no main outflow—more of a cataract than a waterfall. The resultant voice of the onrush is not singular in pitch, but layered and melodic, soothing yet spirited. *This is Paradise,* you exclaim, and I nod in compliance. *Yes, this is Paradise!*

Two: The Rapidan Club

I do not think that the measure of a
civilization is how tall its buildings are,
but rather how well its people have
learned to relate to their
environment and fellow man.
Sun Bear

In 1931 there were two buildings of notable stature constructed. One was the Empire State Building in New York City; the other, located one thousand miles away in Northern Ontario, was a small log cabin on the Trout Streams, deep in the Temagami wilderness. Two disparately different structures, each delegating the consciousness of an era saddled by an ever-increasing consumer-based society, stood resolute and firm in their respective purposes. The Empire State Building, pretentious in its almost obscene dimension, the Altar of Mammon built on the back of a nation in economic and social ruin, was a crude attempt by politicians to rekindle the faith in a capitalist democracy. The Cabin, on the other hand, was constructed primarily for its owner to escape the madness and tedium represented by such overt and politically motivated initiatives.

It was also the year that infamous author, cum wildlife conservationist, Grey Owl, wrote his most endearing book, *Men of the Last Frontier,* effectively capturing the essence of northern Canada's backwoods lifestyle. This Englishman, who postured as a Canadian Indian, learned his bush skills from local Temagami trappers and Bear Island Reserve Aboriginals. Working as a fishing and canoeing guide in 1925 to 1926, Archie Belaney (his real name), in all likelihood plied the waters of the highly touted Trout Streams before The Cabin was built by the "Wrecking Crew."

With logs hewn from the site, the seven "Bear Island Boys," known locally as the "Wrecking Crew," headed by guides Presque Petrant and his brother Dan (descendants of a French-Canadian Métis Bear Island Post packateer) constructed the 14 x 20 foot cabin in three weeks. The black spruce logs were

Archie Belaney (aka Grey Owl), famous Canadian/English author who portrayed himself as an Indian and learned his trade as trapper and outdoorsman while paddling in Temagami in the early 1900s.

felled and peeled in the spring, when the bark comes off easily in long ribbons without the need of a drawknife. The forest at the site was recovering from a recent fire, and the absence of large trees allowed the sun to dry the stacked logs in short order. Planking for the roof, hardwood for the floors, rolls of asphalt roofing, several windows, hardware, chairs and two wood stoves were brought in the previous winter by dogsled, a 48-kilometre (about 30 miles) trip north from Bear Island Reserve. With the influx of tourists flooding north to Lake Temagami, and the need for caretakers and handymen, the Wrecking Crew took easily to the art of woodworking and cabin building.

Even with the Stock Market crash of 1929 and the Depression years of the early 1930s, Lake Temagami had quickly become the "Hollywood" of the north—a destination for those escaping financial misfortune; it also attracted those wilderness interlopers who could afford to pay for services. The "Cobalt Special" rail service pushed north in 1903 to connect with the small village of Temagami, located at the very eastern terminus of the lake. It was a sixteen-hour train ride from Toronto to Temagami, giving its occupants the impression that they had ventured as far north in North America as was possible. In 1927, the Ferguson Highway afforded a bumpy three-hour drive from North Bay, bringing with it burgeoning tourist traffic. Log lodges were constructed amongst the giant pines while socialites were conveyed aboard a variety of tour boats and motor launches. The Hudson's Bay Company Trading Post at Bear Island became a major tourist destination. Lake Temagami was the furthest one could travel north to see *real* Indians in their natural habitat; and while Native Canadians were beheld as one might view an animal in a zoo cage, the loss of wilderness and aboriginal culture was an implacable reality lurking beyond the hoopla.

Hollywood took advantage of the accessible Temagami wilderness, filming *The Silent Enemy* in 1928—a silent flick capturing Indian life using local actors (the last silent movie to be made in North America). Lucille Ball and Bob Hope visited Lake Temagami during the same year. James Cagney starred in *Captain of the Clouds,* a film about a bush pilot and flying stunts carried out by ace First World War pilot Billy Bishop. The first run of *Last of the Mohicans* hailed the abilities of local guides and aspiring Native actors. Arthur Judson, president of CBS and spouse Rita Hayworth, opened Camp White Bear in 1929, located in the south arm of Lake Temagami, entertaining such noble celebrities as Cary Grant, Clark Gable and wife Carole Lombard, and, of course, Jimmy Stewart whose uncle already owned a cabin on the lake.

During this time, Cleveland, Ohio, home of the prodigal mother of "rock & roll," molded a fraternal bond with the Temagami wilderness. Joe Spitzig and his Cleveland partners bought the impressive three-storey log lodge, the Temagami Inn, in 1920: his royal guests included the burlesque troupe, Rockettes (known then as the Roxyettes), made famous through their popular New York Roxy Theatre and Radio City Hall performances. Perched on the cusp of raw wilderness, the Temagami Inn was no two-bit rooming house. The Inn boasted of 100 canoes and a solid mahogany motor launch, powered by a sixteen-cylinder Rolls Royce engine; there were riding horses, tennis courts, a square- (and ballroom) dance hall, card-playing room, barber shop and marine lounge. For nimrods aching to catch trophy lake trout or shoot moose and bear, there were twenty-five guides lined up like caddies at a private golf resort. Bear Island guides, or even wannabe Indians like Archie Belaney, aka Grey Owl, might have taken their clients up to the Trout Streams to catch the elusive brook trout.

There were other Cleveland interests, perpetrated by those with a penchant for locking up choice parcels of Canadian real estate. At the time of the uncertain American economy, there was a prevailing *escapist* mentality, and an insatiable desire to own a retreat in the wilderness—*the Canadian wilderness.*

This was not only a cheap proposition, but also a widely engineered phenomenon. Company CEOs, doctors, lawyers and bankers wanted a piece of Temagami turf, and they got it at bargain prices. Islands on the lake were sold, cottages were built by Bear Island carpenters and the local economy blossomed.

Robert Burton Newcomb was the "King" of Temagami. His royal acclamation was consolidated by virtue of his prominence as paddler and part-time resident on Lake Temagami. He earned both a law and medical degree and started his own practice with Cleveland canoe buddies in 1900. Alfred R. Horr joined them in 1904. Horr was the vice-president of the Cleveland Trust Company and president of the Cleveland Chamber of Commerce. These barristerial canoe aficionados trekked north to claim their bit of paradise, staking claim to several islands adjacent to Bear Island even before the Ontario government opened the existing Temagami Forest Reserve for cottaging. The Camp Fire Club of Cleveland, as they branded themselves, must have had some persuasive power over the local magistrates because of their influence, power and the American dollar that flowed freely in Temagami. By 1906 leases were established for those settling in to cottage life on the islands; the entire shoreline of the lake was not to be developed for fear of wild fires caused by careless land clearing and brush burning. Newcomb and friends who had been squatting illegally were now required to build a structure, as prescribed by government regulation, of no less than $300.00 in value; the lease was renewable after twenty-one years. Fees were $20.00 annually for the first half-acre or less, and $3.00 for every additional acre. Newcomb then built a two-storey log cabin on his island—an almost perfect departure point for canoe sojourns through his kingdom.

Newcomb and Horr, during the summer of 1908, paddled an incredible 1,516 kilometres (942 miles) from Lake Temagami to James Bay and back in just five weeks—the first non-natives with no ties to the fur trade to complete this Herculean journey. Archie Belaney had just arrived on the scene and was bonding with the Anishnabek at Bear Island; he was sure to have parleyed with the Camp Fire Boys during one of Bear Island's summer shindigs. Newcomb's forays into the nearby Temagami wilds often took him to the infamous Trout Streams and beyond. These trips were rather grandiose and fanciful. Having obtained the services of one guide per man, including a cook, the Camp Fire Boys left the more arduous chores to the hired help while they ambled over the rocky portages of the river carrying only their own personal gear.

Newcomb wasn't entirely satisfied with just one cottage on Lake Temagami so he acquired several more lots and established ownership under the names of friends and associates. He also began to spend more time with his brother Adrian, a partner in his Cleveland law firm, embarking on several excursions up the south branch of the Trout Streams, surely one of their favourite trips in Temagami. Like Florence Lake, and many other place names of aboriginal origin, the Trout Streams lost their rightful cognomen to philandering politicians who thought it quaint to remove unpronounceable Indian names from the maps, and replace them with the names of nieces, wives, daughters, debutants and whores. Lady Evelyn, to whom the Newcombs now owed the privilege of salutations as they pushed their canoes along her meanders and rock-strewn rapids, or portaged around precipitous cataracts, was the wife of the Duke of Devonshire—Governor General of Canada from 1916 to 1921, *and* daughter of the 5th Marquess of Lansdowne—Governor General of Canada from 1883 to 1888. Not one of these bluebloods had ever set foot on any parcel of turf in Temagami, nor humped a load on any one of the river's brutal portages, or been burdened with pack or canoe amidst a scourge of blackflies, mosquitoes, deer flies, horseflies or midges, and, most astonishingly, never knew that such a place even existed. Those who have accomplished this adventure often remark that Lady Evelyn *was no lady at all.*

The brothers formed a syndicate in 1930, which included a handful of their closest associates—at least those with any semblance of "sporting blood" who were capable paddlers, able to surmount the many gruelling portages up the river. The Rapidan Exploration Syndicate Limited was probably chartered over tin cups of Canadian bootleg whisky, shared on a portage one snowy day, up on the Lady Evelyn in September of 1929. Adrian Newcomb and his wife Helen, Robert and his wife Faith, camped at the "Flume," now known as "Fat Man's Falls" (because of the narrow crevice of rock one has to squeeze through while loaded down with canoe or pack), hunkering down behind one of their overturned canoes, their campfire spitting out warmth, and pondered the idea of building a cabin somewhere up on the Lady Evelyn.

Location of the cabin would not be an easy decision; rapids, chutes, canyons and falls choked the entire south branch of the river. There was a paucity of actual building sites because of the tenuous, broken landscape, except for a few terraces of rock that fronted each of the three falls. The major difficulty

would be transporting construction materials in to such a remote location; one solution would be to take down local trees for use as log walls and rafters, and either fly in or haul all other supplies in by float plane or dog team. Still, no matter where they decided to build, it would be a monumental task to carry out. They chose the first waterfalls, slightly over three kilometres (about two miles) from Divide Lake where they could land a plane and have the shortest distance to carry goods in by hand and canoe. There were plenty of good, straight trees and a superb vista looking north up the rapids; the falls pitched out of sight just beyond the pools in front of the proposed site so the noise level would be tolerable, not deafening. Once they were committed to the site, it was just a matter of hiring the Wrecking Crew to do the labour.

The cabin would be named after Herbert J. Hoover's favourite fishing camp on the Rapidan River, located in the Virginia Mountains. The Newcombs admired the president's spontaneous departures from civic life, as he headed up to the headwaters of the Rapidan whenever the urge took him, and always when the trout were biting. Robert, in particular, began to spend more and more time in Temagami, away from the tedium of his practice in Cleveland. The Rapidan Camp on the Lady Evelyn was the two brothers' ultimate dream escape.

Permits, deeds and surveys would legitimize the Camp at a later date when someone in the local forestry office would actually take notice. At the time, squatting was fairly commonplace, and if you had connections, or were doing incidental "favours" for provincial premiers (as the Newcomb brothers were purported to have been doing), then the validation of such enterprises was an insignificant triviality. Also, being lawyers, the Newcombs were well aware of the lax system of land disposition in Ontario.

Robert began keeping a cabin journal. Black and white photographs were meticulously interspersed with journal notes, about weather, about trips up the river from their Lake Temagami cottage with his wife, sometimes with the boys. In it also were newspaper clippings: "Rapidan Calls Hoover"; "President Suddenly Leaves for Rapidan"; "Hoover Hears Call of Trout." One clipping stands out, particularly a quote as follows:

> Probably because people are not so terribly interested in material things as many imagine. A man is always a boy. He dreams of forests and streams and rushing torrents and all that invites him back to a care free boyhood. He, too, would step into a canoe with Indians of a summer's morning and disappear around the bend down the river, because adventure is in the heart of every man. To chase moose out of a stream, to see a fight between antlered bucks, to note the flight of birds, to make friends with beaver and bear—to portage into lakes no one has ever seen before, to visit a pagan tribe, to be friends with voyageurs and trappers and prospectors and listen to their strange tales around the camp fire—these things grip the mind of men, whose fate is to spend their lives among the brick and stone.

Robert Newcomb, modest in his own effectuation as a writer, probably wrote this himself without assigning ownership, maybe for the express enjoyment of substantiating some sort of personal credo espoused by a greater power outside of but familiar with his domain. Robert tried his best to assimilate into a backwoods lifestyle without completely letting go of all the strings of security anchored in the corporate infrastructure that defined him. He and his wife were generous to the Bear Island Indians, often visiting their trapping grounds in the winter; hauled out by dog team by guides John Turner or Presque Petrant, they would travel the Temagami winter wilds for three weeks at a time. Newcomb championed their causes and formulated a union between Native and cottager through the creation of the Temagami Lakes Association. He became the organization's first president. During the winter, it wasn't unusual for the Newcombs to host visits from Bear Island families wanting to get a taste of Cleveland city life. As if trying to close the gap between two cultures, Newcomb encouraged Natives to assimilate more to modern white ways so he could lessen the distance needed for him to be at their place of peace.

But the wilderness can have a deleterious effect on a person's psyche, particularly with those who have an infatuation with a lifestyle they can never attain. An affair with wilderness, to live simply with the denizens of the forest, can be a fool's dream. Newcomb had a foot set in each camp; perennially affixed to Cleveland by profession and responsibility, yet tied inextricably to Temagami through spirit. His convictions eventually became muddled; he became morose and angry; truths lapsed into lies, hope betrayed rational thought, and unrequited love of a simpler life eventually pushed his heart into the depths of despair. Wilderness, the temptress, has been known to seduce the most steadfast of men with its beauty and its informality: *the Calling* drawing them away from home with romantic persuasion—*the trail life,* free from the pangs of listlessness, released from the clutches of unvarying duty, the perturbations of constricting family life—*the beckoning of absolute freedom*!

On March 19, 1934, at the age of sixty-one, Robert Newcomb calmly, quietly, picked up his splitting axe he kept in his Cleveland garage, went inside the house and brutally murdered his wife Faith. Then, with the deft, sure hand of a surgeon, he cut his own throat with a straight razor.

The murder-suicide shocked Bear Islanders, so much so that, despite the circumstances, they erected a stone monument to Newcomb on the grassy front lawn of the Hudson's Bay Company store.

The Cabin, barely three years old, stood empty. The enthusiasm of the Rapidan Club waned cold like a winter moon; suddenly, the distance and the work it took to get there became too much for the remaining syndicate members. Paradise lost. Vacant of any more than a few pages of fanciful banter and postcard photographs, Newcomb's cabin journal retired to obscurity amongst the mothballs and memorabilia of a family trunk.

Three: The Pine Tree

We should talk less and draw more.
Personally, I would like to renounce
speech altogether and, like organic
nature,communicate everything
I have to say in sketches.
Goethe, 1749-1832

The *Cabin* was built the same year my mother was struck by lightning while crossing a streetcar track in Hamilton, near Toronto. She was ten years old. Thirty years later, when I turned ten, I found myself standing at the foot of the largest tree I had ever seen. It was a white pine tree, massive, gnarled—bigger than any other tree that edged our property. It was at the top of a hill, beside a farmer's field, somewhere along the southern rise of the Oak Ridges Moraine, thirty miles north of Toronto. The pine tree was bereft of branches for the first fifty feet of its height at which point it blossomed into a canopy of green, limbs stretching outwards like the underside of an umbrella. There were stubs of branches all the way up its wide trunk, none of which looked safe enough to be used as a foothold; also attached was a decrepit ladder made of cut boards, spaced about two feet apart and running the full height as far as the lowest limbs. The tree had either grown around the boards or pushed them out from the trunk, hanging where they had rotted away from the spikes that once held them tight. Compelled to climb, I put my hand on the second rung. It felt sturdy. Butterflies swarmed in my belly as I stepped up on the first board. It was loose. When I reached for the third rung, I lost my purchase on the first board as it cracked and broke, sending me tumbling on the bed of pine needles below the tree. Frustrated but not defeated, I knew I would be back.

BULLET MISSES BABY BY INCHES, ASLEEP IN PRAM
Willowdale, April 29, 1952—*Toronto Star*
Sleeping in his carriage, a seven-month-old baby narrowly missed being struck by a .22 rifle bullet yesterday on the back veranda of his

parents' Yorkview Drive home, North York, police said today. The bullet, which police said was fired by a youth a quarter of a mile away, pierced the rear door of the home of Norman Wilson. The bullet passed within inches of the baby's carriage and landed on the floor near the feet of Mrs. Wilson who was preparing the evening meal. Police said Gordon Westall, 16, of Horsham Avenue, told them he was shooting at starlings in his father's henhouse.

If ever there was a prophetic event, this was it. Life from here would be a series of narrow escapes. The presumed sanctity afforded by my filial abode was dubiously suspect. Not that our home at the northern edge of Toronto continued to be a target for aspiring young hunters, my parents never quite got the hang of parenting. Aside from the socially required obligation to supply to your offspring the necessary food, shelter and clothing to survive, my parents were lacking in any deep, organic emotion. Love, as an endearing expression of childcare, was as misguided as a stray bullet.

My assignment of parents did ascribe to some interesting historical genetic discipline. My mother was of French Huguenot descent, artists, philosophers and musicians, they were chiefly Protestants who took a liberal stand on social reform, sparred openly with the Roman Catholic autocracy, and eventually found themselves heading for distant hills to avoid persecution. My anarchistic precursors fled to England where they became horse thieves. My father's gene pool was even more provocative; of Scottish descent, the Wilson/Gunn highlanders raped, pillaged and plundered with peculiar efficiency. The mad Scotts were progeny of the Norsemen—those gallant interlopers who crashed their boats into Canadian turf, some 500 years before Christopher Columbus stole all the fanfare.

Trying to rationalize why I strayed from the proverbial *beaten path,* spending the better part of my life in search of personal sanctuary, prompted a clarity of understanding what was happening in the world at the time my life nearly ended in 1952. Here I was, perched on the back porch of a small post-war home, dodging bullets, when the United States invaded Korea and TV was transforming American society. An ever-paranoid U.S. government had stepped up its A-bomb testing in Nevada to keep pace with the Russians and radioactive "snow" had been detected along the shores of Lake Ontario, settling, no doubt, on my blankets as I slept soundly in my pram on the back porch. Of course, the Atomic Energy Commission denied that nuclear testing would "conceivably produce any damage to humans" and for a citizen to launch a complaint was overtly unpatriotic.

Nuclear deposition, statically electrified gene material induced by a rogue lightning blast, crazed Norse blood—that cocktail shaker of genetic stratum conjoined somehow to manifest in my own personality: such qualities assuredly forecasting a narrow and uncertain trail through the dark Tolkien woods ahead. My parents were not at all religious except for the doctrines outlining child discipline where "spare the rod and spoil the child" was precursor to Dr. Spock's notion that beating your child may have future repercussions.

My grandmother had a cottage on Clear Lake, in the Kawartha District of Ontario, about a two-hour drive northeast of Toronto. My brother and sister, along with a mélange of cousins, aunts and unemployed uncles, would spend summers there. Anyone under the age of twelve would be banished to the boathouse at sundown while parents played bridge and drank themselves into a stupor. The boathouse served well as our childhood sanctuary, where games were played and the lapping of water against the shore lulled night dreams. In the slow hour of breaking dawn we would wake to the sound of thrushes, whippoorwills and mourning doves.

I was six when I met old Charlie—an Ojibwa elder woodsman from the Curve Lake Reserve. He was hired by my father to consult and act in a survival movie he was filming for the Department of Lands and Forests. It was being filmed in the woods behind our cottage. When Charlie wasn't working he would take my brother and me into the bush to teach us camp craft, not the ersatz skills found in Boy Scout journals, but *real* Indian lore, like boiling water in a birchbark bowl, "reading" sign where there were no trails and, best of all, how to paddle a canoe. I was still afraid of the water since my father had thrown me off the end of the dock and I nearly drowned, so I would watch from shore while the other older kids paddled, or my father and uncle would put me in the middle of the canoe while they paddled. I remember stealing glances over the gunwale, cautiously, thinking that the weeds would reach up and pull me into the lake.

Charlie was the embodiment of things magical. He said little, but his gestures and mannerisms were refreshingly genuine and gentle-natured. And when I didn't understand, or I did something that wasn't correct, he would smile or laugh and show me again as if we had all the time in the world. He was a large, stocky man, dark-skinned with greased-back black hair, and he always wore green trousers with a red-checkered lumberjack shirt. Charlie smelled of the earth, pungent woodsmoke and wet moss, quite unlike the fusty malodour of my own family, a concoction of Vitalis, Player's cigarettes, Labatt 50, Canadian Club and mothballs. The way Charlie did things was spellbinding: the way he spun the canoe in tight circles, the soundless way he drifted through the woods like an owl on the wing—always with a modicum of effort, always with unreserved pleasure. I was mesmerized—*I wanted to be Indian too.*

My father, on the other hand, along with the coterie of male role models that showed up on the weekends to fish and drink beer, designed their own failures with peculiar regularity. The afternoon my father sank the cottage skiff became a lake legend; he did learn that you can't shoot a muskie in the head with a .410 survival pistol while the fish is sitting on the bottom of the boat. A cottage ritual, which I now find utterly repugnant, was the bagging of cottage garbage which was barged out into the middle of the lake and dumped—a typical practice executed by most part-time summer residents of cottage country. But for two months of the year I found sanctuary in the thin walls of a wooden boathouse, fermenting visions of Indian life, for a brief moment forgetting the fact that for the ten remaining months of the late 1950s, home was nothing more than a battleground for my parents.

I was nine when we moved north. It was a large property, forested, framed by farmers' fields and undeveloped forest—ripe for the explorations of a little boy. The immediate task was to build a fort—an occupation kids seem to take on with committed zeal, pleasure and complicity. I was no different; but for obvious reason, the need to construct something *solid* around me prompted a fixation on detail that always required a surfeit of energy. *My* forts needed to be impregnable, and if they weren't built to keep people out, they were then constructed in absolute secrecy so that no other neighbour kid, and certainly *no adult,* could find them. And there was a preternatural progression from simple "hideout," which was fabricated out of whatever material was close at hand—sticks, bark, relic plywood, plastic or metal—to a more elaborate design that required a respect for the *process.* Some thought, calculation, effort and time had proven results. Instead of simply gathering excreta from Nature or human industry, and tossing it together accidentally, the employment of tools consecrated a resounding pledge to self-fulfillment.

First attempts were clouded by misadventure and near death. Digging in the steep side of a sand embankment near our new house, with the help of a boy who lived up the road, we bored a hole about eight feet deep and wide

HAP WILSON 2001

enough to squirm into on our bellies. It suddenly caved in on us. Luckily, I was near enough to the entrance to pull myself out, but my friend had disappeared under tons of sand. I could hear him screaming inside. Clawing away at the bank with my bare hands, scooping the sand like a mad dog, I reached his feet. The sand was packed hard around his legs, but if I stopped I knew he would be dead in a matter of minutes. Once his hips were free I was able to pull him out while he squirmed and pushed. We were both crying, scared out of our wits. Two weeks after this incident I heard that three local boys had died in a collapsed tunnel they were digging.

It was clearly defined that tunnels were definitely not the way to go. Chumming up with my brother and two neighbourhood boys, we loaded up a wagon with tins of salvaged nails, assorted hand tools and crossed the highway into unknown territory. By nightfall we had constructed a crude lean-to. Without flashlights or even a moon to guide us, we headed back towards the highway and home. It was pitch black. I crossed the highway first with the others close behind. I could still hear their voices. That's when the car without headlights on hit us at high speed.

I remember an explosion of sound, and a lightshow of sparks and flashes that rivalled any Dominion Day fireworks celebration. *The car must have hit the wagon,* I thought as I hit the ground, tools and shrapnel whizzing by my head. *My brother!* It took some time to collect what had happened but miraculously, no one was injured. A split second before the car hit, the boy towing the wagon heard the vehicle barrelling down the road at them and managed to jump aside. My brother and the other boy followed suit. The man in the car was furious at us but retracted when we told him we were calling the cops if he didn't buy us a new wagon. Two days later, a brand new Radio Flyer was sitting on my friend's porch.

I explored my world farther from home. As my parents fought, the trips became more frequent, often taking up whole days. That's when I found the pine tree. And that behemoth stood there in stark relief, taunting, demanding to be climbed—the view from the top would be nothing shy of spectacular. I would put my hand on the first rung of the decrepit ladder trying to build up enough courage to go up, but there was always something holding me back. Always.

The Oak Ridges Public School was a place of social and hierarchical selection: girls slipped you candy bars if they liked you, bullies beat you up if a popular girl slipped you a candy bar at recess, and gangs pitched battle with endless fury. Teachers kept the leather strap out in full view, usually perched on the corner of their desk. Any self-willed or intractable student requiring discipline had to step out into the hall where the strap was administered; sobs, whimpering and pleas to stop, matched with the resounding *SNAP* of coarse leather against the plump skin of soft wrists, echoed hauntingly through the corridors and into open-doored classrooms.

Eddy was my salvation. He was the grandson of our neighbour next door. Ed's parents had divorced so he spent weekends at his grandpa's. He was a strangely quiet boy, powerfully built for an eleven-year-old. Like me, he liked Indians, so we slowly, methodically, and irretrievably transmogrified ourselves into red-skinned savages from Friday night to Sunday afternoon until Ed was hustled back to Toronto to go to school. We began living for the weekends and dreamt about what we would do on holidays. In the fall of 1963 we began building the stockade. We would build the *piece de resistance* of all forts, a place where we could live outdoors and live in virtual solitude away from the madding crowd.

And so it was agreed upon that we would indeed construct a stockade of goodly proportions, crafted stability and absolute security. A suitable location was selected behind Ed's grandpa's house, half on their property and half on ours—about forty-six metres (fifty yards) from my nemesis, the pine tree. It was some distance from our house, thankfully, because my parents frowned on such activities, but being in view of Ed's grandparents' house afforded easy access to tools, water and prepared lunches supplied by his grandmother. The stockade would also incorporate an existing tree house that had already served us well as a place to camp out in.

A rough perimeter of about sixty metres (about two hundred feet) in circumference was scribed on the ground, taking advantage of existing trees that would be necessary to anchor the wall sections of the palisade. To a couple of twelve-year-olds the size of the planned stockade looked immense, calculating the number of logs that would be required to close in the space outlined. With unbound alacrity we set out to collect logs, dead ones mostly, anything of the right girth, strength and length—about three metres (ten feet) long— and then dragged, hauled or carried them over our shoulders back to the building site. Our collected pile grew slowly, with agonizing astonishment at the amount of work demanded of us and the distance wc had to lug the heavy logs. Before long, we were liberating logs from over a kilometre away, and even though we knew we needed at least a thousand of them to complete the palisade, we were immortal in our quest to get the job done.

Once the walls started to appear, the visual reference point made it easier to procure logs from distant places. Stanchions were planted where there wasn't a tree to anchor on to; walls went up in sections of almost three metres (just over three yards) each—the distance between supports; each sharpened pole was snubbed in the ground and tied with binder twine to cross-ties, and methodically it all started appearing as if we could actually pull it off. Progress was interminably slow but deliberate, slower near the end of completion because of the distance we travelled to scrounge for logs. On one foray that took me at least two-and-a-half kilometres away, two boxer dogs on the loose attacked me. They were feeding on kitchen waste dumped by the local golf clubhouse and obviously mistook me as a rival. Luckily I had an old machete strapped to my belt which, when pulled, managed to scare them off. But my leg had been badly mauled in the scuffle. I triumphed over the resultant scar that reminded me always of my own tenacity—it's not so much of a vicious dog bite but as the memory of building the stockade.

During the Cuban missile crisis, when we learned at school to hunker down beneath our desks in case of a nuclear explosion (prompted not to look at the bright flash), my father had my brother and me excavate a hole underneath the house for a fallout bunker. This, among other seemingly senseless chores, kept me away from completing the stockade. There was a resident and nationally pervasive aura of insecurity and paranoia within each household across America that filtered down into its children. The death of President Kennedy and the doom and gloom of world events consolidated that fear that I remember so well. It was all on TV, in vivid black and white. Life in the outdoors, away from the craziness of the world run amuck by a generation of zealots, fanatics, despots and dictators, for me, cemented a lifelong distrust of the "system."

I climbed about six metres (twenty feet) up the pine tree when my legs began to shake uncontrollably. It was much harder going down. I sat at the bottom looking up, watching the clouds roll by, wondering why this was so hard for me to do. I wasn't really afraid of heights, but I didn't trust someone else's handiwork. Antiquated as it was, the ladder petrified me. I loved that tree but hated myself for my faint-heartedness.

In 1964, the Beatles conquered the world with music, and no doubt it was a welcomed retreat from the reality of Vietnam. Regardless of how the United States government obfuscated the brutality and omnipresent force of a political agenda gone awry, the verity of such hedonistic events that dominated television, radio and newspaper, filtered into our lives like battery acid on clothing, eating away at the very fabric of trust. Faith that things would change anytime soon was elusive—all the more reason to finish the stockade, soon. *That* was my reality, and the fact that I was now a teenager—one more step closer to freedom. I would now lose myself in my drawings or in long hikes through the woods with Ed, and every once in a while, stare up into the heavenly shade of the giant pine tree with ever-flourishing transparency of thought.

It took Ed and me over a year to complete the stockade. Hawthorn bramble was secured to the outside of the palisade to dissuade anyone from cutting down the walls, and a lockable gate was hung on leather hinges. Ed had built most of the teepee by the time I had returned from a nightmare, cross-country road trip with my parents. I helped with the furnishings and finishing touches. There was a roll-down door flap and flip-over smoke hatch with a fire pit ringed with stones, while beds were built around the back half-circle base of the teepee, using cut poles raised about a foot off the ground. Spruce boughs were collected for bedding. It was finished—almost two years after we had started.

My parents abhorred the idea of me sleeping outside. When they forbade me to go, like any teenager I would find a detour, and in this case it meant sneaking out of my bedroom window late at night and returning for breakfast at dawn, before anyone else awoke. This went on for two more years, even through the winter months. Ed would be there with the fire going, waiting, whittling something or reading. The mouldy, damp sleeping bag that had started to grow its own verdant life forms became a chattel of freedom representing the simplicity of a non-combatant, peaceful escape. I slept soundly while the fire cracked and snapped, and the smoke pall inside the teepee crept downward, halting inches above our dormant bodies.

We ran wild. Two boys dressed in fabricated loincloths, half-naked, sharing the secret language of the wilderness, hunting, learning and living out our wild imaginings. I could *feel* the wildness of my own body touching the earth on my bare feet, and the coolness of the wind on my face as I ran through the woods. *This is what life was all about,* I thought.

My father had an argument with Ed's grandfather about property lines. Mostly it was the fact that Gramps kept making passes at my mother. The dispute was vicious; in the end we had to move the stockade so that it was on the neighbour's land. Every stick was transported to the new location; not an easy task except that we didn't have to search for more logs. A roomier wigwam was built, along with a target for our throwing 'hawks—a pastime we had learned to perfect over the past couple of years. Little did I know that this skill, thirty years later, would land me in Hollywood as Pierce Brosnan's personal trainer for the Attenborough film, *Grey Owl.*

I was fifteen when I climbed the tree. I was strong and determined, but most of all afraid that if I didn't climb the tree soon I would not have the courage to stand true to my beliefs and aspirations. As to what these were, was not clearly defined for me except that I knew what I didn't want out of life. And so, one day after much deliberation, while my parents fought, I marched out of the house and climbed the steep hillside to the back of the property, to a place I knew well by this time. Without thinking at all about anything but the top of the tree and how beautiful life must look from there, I climbed. And I climbed without looking down, without hesitation, tears streaming from my cheeks and with a will of purpose so strong that I must have frightened the demons that sat on every rung of that aged ladder until finally, with uninhibited joy, I reached the first branch of that mother pine and pulled myself into her embrace. Slowly I made my way up, snakelike, working my body through the maze of scaly limbs, the trunk diminishing in breadth until I found a perch near the very top, never looking down. When I stopped climbing I could then feel the tree moving, swaying in the wind. But it was the music in the way the wind caressed the pine boughs that touched my soul; gentle voices, like old

Charlie the Ojibwa woodsman, telling me things would be all right. When I chanced a look out from my sky haven, when the moths in my gut had settled and the wind had lulled, I drew in a breath and opened my eyes. *I could see Toronto!* Sure enough, the skyline was purely visible some fifty kilometres (about thirty miles away), Lake Ontario drifting like a haze behind the heat waves. For me it was an epiphany to have climbed the tree, rising above my self-doubts and inhibitions, to see clearly the path that lay ahead. Nothing would be as hard as climbing that tree, or as illuminating as the exaltation of such accomplishment. The climb down was another thing.

Four: Hyde's Cabin and The Dirty Dozen Club

It's a good time to have a beer.
Franklin Delano Roosevelt, 1934
(end of Prohibition)

As the western world reeled on the heels of the Great Depression, Hitler's Nazi regime escalated. The complacent "Jazz Era" of the 1920s sidled into the 1930s under a dark cloud of fear and paranoia. As of September 10, 1939, Canada joined England in the war against Germany while the United States remained neutral. At least half of the cottages on Lake Temagami were American owned—a major component of the local economy. Canada, along with a coterie of Temagami businessmen—the ever-so-urbane host—made every effort to trivialize any evidence of the war so that American tourists continued to enjoy the Canadian woods, unconscious of the fact that the country was at war. The executives of the Cottager's Association, founded by R.B. Newcomb in 1931, made it clear to Americans that "the hostilities abroad would make no difference in daily life on Lake Temagami, despite strict rationing and controlled prices at the grocery store."

It wasn't until December 7, 1941, when Japan attacked Pearl Harbor, that the social mood changed on the lake; cocktail banners were removed from boathouse flag poles, cottages boarded up and enrolment in camps and inns dropped so low that many didn't even open. Since the wartime association president, Harry Schumaker, a real estate developer from Buffalo, New York, had a cottage on the lake, it would be difficult and unsavoury for any American tourist to lag behind in paradise.

Adrian Newcomb continued to visit Rapidan on the Lady Evelyn, but the visits became sporadic and lonely ventures, misted in sad recollections. By 1940 he was hard pressed to coerce anyone else to go with him so he sold a one-half interest to the cabin to his friends, Howard and Katherine Hyde, in return for some much needed restoration of the property. The Hyde's son, Alan, paddled and portaged a stack of 2 x 12s and a four-ton jack over the little more than three-kilometre (two-mile) portage from Diamond Lake up to the Trout Stream on his way to repair the cabin porch. Such dedicated industry prompted Adrian to sell his remaining share to the Hydes in 1949. Rapidan Camp became known quietly as "Hyde's Cabin;" the falls, which had been nameless until then, became known as "Cabin Falls." Adrian's final trip to The Cabin was in 1951, the year that I was born in Toronto.

Max and Richard Lathrop were born and raised in Brocton, New York, an inconspicuous hamlet located some sixty-four kilometres (forty miles) south of Buffalo. Max eventually opened up his own restaurant on the shore of Lake Erie, near the small town of Barcelona, sixteen kilometres (ten miles) south of Brocton. Lathrop's Lakeview Restaurant did well in the late 1940s post-war boom. Richard had a number of professions, the lengthiest of which posted him as the owner of the state theatre in Falconer, New York, a subdivision of Jamestown about forty-eight kilometres (thirty miles) from Brocton. Richard often let his two sons, Dan and Jim, sell tickets and popcorn, and occasionally run the giant projector. Richard later became business manager for the Falconer Central School District. Both Max and Richard were members of the fraternal brotherhood of Freemasons. Neither one travelled much but there was one place they would visit at least twice a year, and that was the Temagami wilderness.

Sometime in the late 1940s, the Lathrops teamed up with ten other Jamestown area Freemasons and formed the "Dirty Dozen Club." It was an eclectic association of lower western New York State's most upstanding citizens—mostly fire chiefs and reputable private business owners. When they weren't doing their civic duties or pandering to the public, they gathered at one or the other fire halls to drink vodka and talk about their next hunting or fishing trip. Aside from owning a deer hunting camp in the low hills bordering Pennsylvania, the Dirty Dozen boys owned a cabin in Temagami. The camp was perched on a high-banked sand island in the centre of Lady Evelyn Lake—the lake into which the Lady Evelyn River flowed. Most of the islands were actually glacial-formed eskers, and when the dam was constructed at the outflow of the lake, raising the water levels by nine metres (thirty feet), the islands began to erode. The dam had allowed local logger, Jim Murphy, to boom logs off the lake to the Montreal River and on to the mill in Latchford. Murphy also built his own dams further in to access the pine-rich shores of Diamond Lake. The resident Anishnabek families suddenly found themselves, their belongings and five thousand years of history under almost two metres (six feet) of water. Murphy simply told the Indians, "They had no right to the land."

The dams had a deleterious effect on the Lady Evelyn Lake riparian environment. *Mons-kaw-naw-ning* or "haunt of the moose," as Lady Evelyn Lake had been know to the local Anishnabek for centuries, lost much of its resident charm and appeal as sandbanks eroded and the pine tipped ungraciously into the black water. The Dirty Dozen Camp, regardless of valiant attempts at shoring up the foundation posts, slowly, deliberately, succumbed to gravity and tumbled into the lake.

The Lathrops, though irritated about losing the camp, were still enthralled with the region. Maple Mountain, or *Chee-bay-jing*—"place where soul spirits dwell," a burial site and vision quest mountain for Bear Island Indians, lay prominently in the western horizon as a symbolic guidepost to *deep wilderness.* Until then, the Lathrops fished the local waters, never out of sight of this mountain icon, wondering what lay beyond the rise.

In 1951, with a local Native guide named "Tom," Max and Richard embarked on an exploratory trip up the Trout Streams. The Lathrops may have rubbed shoulders with Adrian Newcomb in the coffee shop at the Ronoco Hotel in Temagami while waiting for the guide to show up. This adventure was an arduous undertaking even for the fit, but the lure of natural brook trout in their pristine waters was enough to light the fire under the two brothers.

Heading towards the Rock Knob uplands, beyond the infamous Maple Mountain, (An ancient burial site, the mountain has witnessed ten deaths, and it is known to be a place of strange happenings where foul weather frequently breaks over its lofty ridge.) the trio ascended the north channel of the Lady Evelyn River, portaging around Frank, Center and Helen Falls consecutively. Center Falls was known well to canoeists who dubbed it the "Golden Staircase," aptly named for its cataracts, ledges and natural sluiceways; the campsite facing the falls was revered as one of the best in Temagami. The *Nastawgan*, an elaborate webwork of interconnecting aboriginal trails, had been used continuously for the past five thousand years. Max and Richard soon learned why local paddlers cringed when the name "Lady Evelyn" was mentioned—the steep, awkward trails around the falls were legion amongst Lake Temagami campers as the most difficult in the region. At Divide Lake, the Lathrops swung back around and down the south channel of the river. When they reached Cabin Falls they were awestruck with the beauty of the place and the unusual presence of a well-built log cabin overlooking the precipice. Standing on the deck in front of the cabin was an old man who politely waved them in for a brew of bush coffee and a shot of Jim Beam. The man's name was Adrian Newcomb, and he explained to the Lathrops that he had built the cabin with his brother Bob back in '31, and that the cabin had been sold recently to the Hyde family. Adrian went on to explain that no one was interested in the difficult trek up the river, and that he himself was too old and sick to act as caretaker for the property. In fact, this was to be his *last* trip to paradise, to Rapidan, and to Temagami.

Before they left Cabin Falls, Adrian informed the Lathrops that the cabin was up for sale if they were interested—*for $600 U.S.!* That was music to the ears of the brothers from Barcelona. Adrian died shortly after the Lathrops returned home; this slowed the mechanics of consolidating a sale but the brothers persevered. Tracking down Katherine Litchfield Hyde who lived in Hudson, New York, was easy—but the purchase did not go through for another six years:

> By transfer 134078 dated 6th June 1957, registered 5th July 1957, made in consideration of $1.00 and other good and valuable consideration Katherine Litchfield Hyde married woman, above named, transferred the above parcel to MAX J. LATHROP & LOUISE A. LATHROP husband and wife of Westfield, in the State of New York, one of the United States of America.

Although the transaction was endorsed by the token dollar and a handshake, Max doled out a paltry six bills in cash to Kate Hyde for the deed. Yearly taxes were less than ten dollars. The Lathrops and the Dirty Dozen Club now had their hands on an outstanding trout camp on the pristine Lady Evelyn River. The Cabin was still in mint condition; aside from the occasional brown paint slapped over the outside walls, there wasn't much to do but collect a bit of driftwood for the fires, catch fish, drink "Old Turkey" on the deck and keep from falling over the edge of the railing into the falls. Not all the members of the DDC were present during their annual spring fishing trip—the cabin was only big enough to sleep eight. And although the trip in was made easier by flying by float plane from the Town of Temagami to Divide Lake, slightly over three kilometres (two miles) upriver, the premise of catching wily brook trout didn't, for most, override the consummate reality of having to slug gear, beer and bait over Canada's worst portages.

Over the next decade, The Cabin had been used for no more than two weeks of the year, usually for the Club's gathering and occasionally by passing canoeists

in need of quick shelter. Maintenance waned as men got older; the cabin began showing traces of its age. Oakum chinking was falling out between the log work, the roof began to leak, the stovepipe was rusting out, deck railings were missing and garbage was being tossed haphazardly over the steep cliffs behind the cabin. To protect their stash of hooch, the Americans put a lock on the door.

In the Canadian northland, for a cabin owner to put a lock on the door was uncustomary; it insulted the honest folk that lived, worked and played in the outdoors. Cabins were commonly left open for those in need of sanctuary, and on a river as wild as the Lady Evelyn where just about anything can happen, knowing there's a warm cabin within close reach could be a lifesaver. Instead, a thick three-inch-wide steel bar was dropped into locking position, pulled up and released by way of a rope and pulley system. The end of the rope was attached to a nail driven in to a plug on the outside of the cabin, beside the door, so all you had to do was work the wooden plug out and yank on the rope to open the door. Since bears were also a problem, heavy gauge rabbit-cage wire was nailed into place covering all the windows. The cabin was now more secure than a liquor store in Lower Detroit.

Divide Lake became a destination for trout fishermen and the Temagami Air Service was more than willing to lighten the pockets of American tourists. Harold Shannon, president of Toronto's Shatco Steel Company and summer cottager on Lake Temagami, grubstaked a man by the name of Glendon

Simms who managed the airways for seven years before his chief pilot, Lou Riopel, bought out his shares. Riopel was without doubt the *chevalier sans peur et sans reproche,* and his deeds did not go unnoticed. *Time Magazine* featured one of his exploits that took place over the frozen bush lands of northern Quebec in 1951. It was the dead of winter and the heavy snow had made flying over the obscure forests and landing on isolated lakes dangerous, mostly because of the slush. Once a ski plane stops, it sinks into the slush, and unless you cut poles and brush to lay out front of the skis, and somehow jack the plane out of the icy slag, the plane will quickly freeze in for the night. There was no GPS satellite technology, or emergency locator beacons that could be set off in emergency situations, and two-way radios were antiquated. A ski plane out of North Bay had gone missing in northwestern Quebec, not far from Temagami.

Riopel, by chance, located the downed plane and circled to have a look. The hapless pilot had spent a frosty night sleeping inside the doorless cabin of his plane until Riopel showed up. Riopel didn't like the looks of the lake and knew that if he stopped, or even taxied slowly, the slush would surely engulf his skis and then there would be two planes down. He decided to land but made a slow run over the snow-covered ice, keeping his ground speed at thirty miles per hour. He made a slow arc around to see if water was filling up the tracks of the skis. It was. Riopel kept his speed up, barely touching the surface of the frozen lake. The pilot from North Bay, seeming to know exactly what was on Riopel's mind, began running toward the moving plane until he was directly alongside of it. He grabbed for a strut and was half dragged down the lake. Riopel hit the throttle when the plane lurched from the extra jolt of the man's weight. Riopel helped the other pilot inside just in time to lift off. Seasoned bush pilots recall that the Temagami pilot successfully carried out the world's first "on-the-fly," ground-to-air rescue. *Ripley's Believe it or Not,* also hailed the daring aviation feat as nothing shy of a modern miracle.

Riopel changed the name of his business to Lakeland Airways. He ran a good business, catering mostly to the "hook & bullet" types, cottagers and camp owners on Lake Temagami. The Trout Streams were popular with the Ohio fishermen and Riopel could always guarantee a successful catch by dropping anglers at Divide Lake on the Lady Evelyn. The cost to fly in was only thirty dollars. Sportsmen plying the pools for trout also had to put up with the scourge of blackflies during peak trout season in late May; tents were pitched and war waged against vexations of flying, buzzing, biting diurnal villains. Eventually, some of the more ardent, bug-bit nimrods would descend the south channel of the river and chance upon The Cabin. Of course the door would be locked, much to the chagrin of the more than curious piscatorians; with bites oozing and self-restraint and composure stretched thin, not even a solid steel bar locking a wooden door could keep out an overwrought man who needed to get out of the bugs. The door would break apart at the hinges and most miscreant visitors wouldn't bother to fix it, or even attempt to shut what was left of it to keep out the varmints. Luckily, the Lathrops had shoved anything of historical value up into the two lofts above the bunks in the cabin—a place nobody dared to poke around in. When things went missing, it was generally the stock of Jim Beam, cutlery, pots or flashlights. And every spring, sure as the arrival of the blackflies, the Lathrops had to mend the door and fix the lock.

By the mid-1960s Max and Richard were past their prime; nearly sixty, they weren't in as good of shape as they had been when they met Adrian Newcomb on the cabin deck fifteen years earlier. The portages seemed longer, the rocks rockier, the weather colder, the bugs nastier and their own resident aches and pains more insistent. Visits to The Cabin became shorter and less frequent. Richard's sons, Dan and Jim, were still young, but he had faith in circumstance that they would want to join him on the annual spring expedition. And they did. But time slowly eroded the putty in the window joints; mice were nesting in the mattresses, the porch had collapsed at the front door, the roof continued to leak into the lofts, the smell of mouse excrement permeated the environment inside so that any food stored, or even prepared, absorbed the aroma of mold and spoilage. Like the Lathrop brothers, The Cabin was feeling its own wretchedness; still, it stood valiant on that mantle of Precambrian rock, seasons flashing by, bereft of human visitors for most of the year, resolute and quaint, slowly composting, slowly dying.

Five: Life Underground

*Everyone has talent. What is rare is the
courage to follow the talent to the dark
place where it leads.*
Erica Jong, b. 1942

"I want to show you something," Ed remarked after my absence from the stockade while on a canoe trip (my first extended canoe venture) with my cousin. Naturally, I was curious; Ed's surprises were always provocative. I sat on my bunk in the wigwam while he began scooping wads of earth from under the middle bed with his cupped hands. He removed a square of plywood that obviously served as some sort of lid for a sunken wooden crate; inside the crate was a steel, army-surplus ammunition box. Taking it out of the crate, he pushed it towards me.

"Look inside," he prompted. I popped open the lid. Inside was a stack of his gramps' *Jaybird* magazines.

"Where'd you get 'em," I inquired with some reservation.

"He threw them out!"

"No shit."

Girls were benignly interesting but I didn't share Ed's enthusiasm; our friendship eventually waned as he began staying in Toronto on weekends. We were growing up and the stockade no longer seemed the appropriate conduit for our quest for adventure or solace. Ed and I embarked on a weeklong summer canoe trip on the Mattawa River—my first taste of whitewater paddling, and although the river, and life on the trail, had apprehended my soul, the trip clearly enunciated the disparate differences we shared about many things. I would not hear from Ed for another thirty-five years.

I started high school in 1965. My parents, by now, had formulated my destiny—a prescription that held no leniency towards unconventional thinking. I had an insatiable craving to draw, but because *it wasn't an honest vocation*—according to my parents—art was definitely out of the question. They sent me to King City High, an alma mater with the dubious dictum *semper progrediens*—always progressing. To what, I thought? There were no art programs, but a surfeit of stricter teachers, a stronger adherence to disciplinary controls and less emphasis placed on physical education. I hated my school; in fact, at the age of fifteen, life had taken such a nose-dive that I began contriving ways to rock the boat in a world that seemed all too orthodox and compliant.

While the Haight Ashbury District of San Francisco, California, was spawning a subculture of young dropouts, namely "Hippies," the Peace, Love and Communal Sharing manifesto migrated north into Canada. LSD was big and banned, Mao Tse-Tung was attacking reactionary bourgeois ideology, and the war in Vietnam was escalating out of control. King City High School, though, never seemed to evolve past the fifties. It was still "Hicksville," Ontario, where the good-looking girls, the cheerleaders and winter carnival queens, dated the "dangerous" guys known colloquially as "greasers." They had the fast cars with the 440-hemi engines. Farm kids stayed home to milk cows or help bring in the hay, while the plurality of students got bussed in from all around. We chanted the Lord's Prayer every morning while staring into the mock smile of Queen Elizabeth, and the tech-teachers beat up, with impunity, the miscreant youths who wouldn't abide by the rules. If a teacher lost the fight, the student was expelled—same as any girl who got herself pregnant. Cars were driven at 120 mph through the country roads, often terminating in a pile of mangled metal and twisted bodies. The school flag would be flown at half-mast and the principal's voice would boom through the school loudspeaker, extolling the virtues of a good Christian, sober teenhood. No Blacks, or students with ethnic persuasions, ever showed up in any classroom in that country school—it was as waspish as one could imagine. Our grade ten history teacher made out with the boys she'd pick up hitchhiking outside the school after four-o'clock. It didn't take long before half the senior boys were lined up with their collective thumbs stuck out, anticipating a ride with "Miss X."

At sixteen I was finally licensed to drive my motorcycle, which I would notoriously park on the steps of the back entrance of the school. That earned me a detention at least once a week, along with detentions for not wearing shoes to class, picking my desk up and turning it toward the windows, or drawing illustrations on handouts that were meant to be taken seriously. Staring at renderings of canoes, trees and birds that filled the borders of one such paper, the principal once looked at me across his desk and remarked with zealous rhetoric how "This would reflect poorly on my future endeavours."

I wasn't listening. And I certainly wasn't alone. Other kids had their own way of rebelling; after all, what we were watching on TV, the blood and the gore of war and the decimation of the Vietnamese culture by the United States, shocked us all into a state of unconsciousness. Few of us trusted either the school authority or our parents. And while many of my peers were searching for their own brand of freedom through drugs, sex, a compulsion to over-achieve, dropping out of school, even suicide, I was resolute on maintaining a firm grip on what was real to me. And that reality was deep-dyed into my psyche by old Charlie the Ojibwa—the sound of rapids, the wail of a loon on a misty lake, the feel of a wooden paddle in my hands, and the dream of my own cabin in the woods. *My own cabin!*

As my parents slipped into an insensible state of malfunction, too busy to care what their children were doing (so long as they marched diligently to the school bus stop every morning), being the pragmatic opportunist and self-indulgent teenager, I hatched the very plan that was conceived as I sat in my perch atop the giant pine tree. *I would some day build my own cabin.* I could feel the life pulsing through the tree, through me as it swayed in the warm summer zephyr—the bark warm against my skin, comforting, like a cheek against a breast. And as I surveyed the world around me, desperately trying to configure my place in it, planning my escape from the madness of family, from school, from the stupidity of global injustice, the only eternal verity, *my axiomatic truth,* compelled me to follow my own path—no matter how righteous it would be perceived.

The summer I drove west with my parents haunts me to this day. Having to take a roadside motel along the trans-Canada highway, out of sheer despera-tion, they wound up in the Native community of Iron Bridge. They would never have stayed in such a "vulgar" establishment since my mother preferred only the most luxurious of hotels, but it was late and we needed to buy gas in the morning. The rookery of Indian hovels pressed up against the back fence of the motel lawn in stark relief. It was hard to believe how anyone could live in such squalor. There was a young Native boy, half my age, across the fence staring at me; he was crying. His face was dirty. He was almost naked. He had been crying for some time because of the obvious tracks the tears had made across his brown cheeks, dried, and then refreshed, again and again. *He was staring through me.* In the background, I could hear loud voices coming from the house. His parents were fighting, viciously: sounds of smashing glass, a TV blared, a dog barked, the sound of a baby crying, doors slammed. Feeling ashamed, scared, confused, I ran back into the motel, away from this lurid, destructive milieu, away from the boy's stare. *They were Indians—they were supposed to be living at peace with the wilderness, with each other.* That day I learned that injustice and social malaise infected much more than my tiny world.

When I started work on my first cabin I was clear-headed about what I wanted to construct. Most of the land around our home was privately owned but still undeveloped and criss-crossed with trails. The cabin had to be virtually invisible. I located a most congenial location across the road from the house, in a large tract of hemlock and pine that belonged to a rather nasty neighbour. This neighbour had taken a personal dislike to me because I would ride my bike through the trails on his property. I chose to build my cabin there, not out of spite for him but because the place was so beautiful to me. I also couldn't imagine why someone would need to own so much property. Selecting a hillock where the sandy soil was deep and firm, I started digging.

An underground cabin? I had no other choice. School was a problem; but I would miss the morning bus, walk to the work site, to my little stash of hand tools, and dig. I went to school just enough to keep up with current studies, borrowing assignments from the A-students and attending to extracurricular athletics so as not to raise suspicion for my culpably negligent attitude. I picked the better weather days to work on the cabin, and the miserable ones to attend school. The only people to know about the cabin project was my friend Glen, who lived in the cluster of houses up the street, and his sister whom I was, in an abstract way, dating, and our mutual friend Kent. Kent was blind. They would sometimes help on the weekends.

The cool autumn air felt good on my bare skin, the smell of damp soil was sweet like overripe apples, and the perspiration fell like tears until I felt totally at peace, exhausted, happy. I'd eat my school lunch and share the bits of crusts with the resident squirrels and curious chickadees. At the end of the day I would stand aside and survey the accomplishments with satisfaction. It was hard to tear myself away from this industry when it came time to get back home, about the time the school bus would drop off the other kids. My parents never knew.

A four-metre (twelve-foot) square hole, two and a half metres (eight feet) deep, was excavated, including a sloped trench that would serve as an entryway. Using an antique crosscut saw, given to me by my uncle, I cut enough stout logs to line the walls. These logs were much bigger than those used for the stockade and the labour involved in locating, milling and carrying prime specimens was

intensive. The walls required almost one hundred logs, set vertically, and nailed together at their crown with a plank header. Slightly smaller logs, about eighty lengths, were milled on the site and fitted into place as rafters, set side-by-each, and sloped at an angle to conform with the lay of the surrounding landscape. Stairs were carved and bolstered with logs within the entranceway, and the walls were lined with cut poles. The gables of the cabin were filled in using salvaged boards, leaving a forty-six centimetre (eighteen-inch) square hole in one end to accommodate a stovepipe thimble. A trapdoor was built and hinged over the entrance, the top camouflaged with bark and sticks; heavy plastic wrap was used to sheath the roof logs and most of the exposed gables. Dirt from the excavation was heaved on top and sculpted to look natural.

I bought an old wood stove for five dollars at the Stouffville Farmer's Market and borrowed my mother's car to haul it back. Glen helped carry it back to the cabin site. With the little extra money I was earning, pruning apple trees for a neighbour, I bought the necessary stovepipe and miscellaneous cabin hardware. In all, the cabin cost less than twenty dollars to build.

The stovepipe was fitted through the sheet-metal thimble I had nailed to the opening in the gable. To conceal the visible, vertical length of pipe, I had located a very large, very hollow pine stump which was pushed and rolled over to the edge of the gable end and propped so as to allow the stovepipe to come up through the centre of it. The top of the stovepipe didn't show; this, however, would later prove to be a problem for draught, doubling the inefficiency of the whole affair of the cabin stove situated in a subterranean cavity where there was no air movement at all. A smoky fire could betray the existence of my sanctuary so it was decided that any fire would be lit of dry scraps of wood only, at a time of dusk or darkness *after* the neighbour and his wife had completed their daily circuit of their property trails. From the outside, the cabin *was* invisible.

To finish off the inside, two pole-and-board bunk beds were built, mattressed with spruce-bough sprigs, covered in old blankets and mildewy old sleeping bags. A couple of decrepit chairs, a crude plywood table and a strip of tattered carpet for the dirt floor furnished the sanctuary. Since there were no windows, with the trap door closed it was darker than a raven's stare inside. A fifty-cent oil lantern maintained a cheery, but half-hearted flush to the cabin walls; the wick, however, could never be properly trimmed which resulted in an annoy-ing strobe-like flicker and a residue of black soot that hung in the cabin like an unwanted guest who wouldn't leave. The scoria from the lantern permeated clothing, bedding and any food that was left on the table and, no doubt, our lungs. After about a month, several species of fungi began to blossom on the walls, hanging like stalactites from the ceiling, dripping with moisture—life from dead logs. Mice, voles, shrews and snakes enjoyed the sanctuary as much as we did. A quick fire would temporarily subdue the biodegradation taking place within the hovel, and we would meet like rebels, explore carnal secrets and drink scorched coffee from cheap tin cups. *It was heaven!*

Six: Cabin Falls

Consider first how slight a shelter
is absolutely necessary.
Henry David Thoreau— *Walden*, 1854

"Your father's very angry with you," my mother warned, as if that was anything new.

"What now," I queried, not knowing what I had done recently to evoke the wrath of the devil.

"The police came to the house while you were away," she remarked rather forcefully, not letting her own emotion be stifled by the presence of my friends sitting in the back seat of the car. I still had no inkling as to what she was eluding to—*the police, why? I hadn't done anything wrong.*

Pooling enough cash, about sixty dollars, to grubstake a month-long canoe trip, I had taken off with three school chums as soon as we got out of school for the year. We were all sixteen years old. It was a remarkable journey covering a distance of over six hundred and forty kilometres (about four hundred miles), ill-equipped and with no maps to speak of. We started in North Bay, paddling downriver on the Mattawa and the Ottawa rivers, and then branching off upstream on the Petawawa River and through Algonquin Park. We should have all died several times along the way. The rapids were fierce and dangerous—we had no life jackets with us; high winds and violent storms plagued the entire trip—we slept under the canoes most of the time; and the hordes of flies were so irksome that we spent many sleepless nights sitting by the fire—we had no insect repellent. At the end of the trip our clothes were so worn out and shoes in such a state of decomposition, that the soles were held on by string tied around our feet. My mother had agreed to pick us up in Algonquin Park where we finished the trip. I was basking in the reverie of self-made adventure, lingering in the camaraderie known only to young boys after defying the odds, drenched in the heavenly bouquet of woodsmoke and sweat—life was brimming full of new experiences.

"Your cabin in the woods…Mr. X wasn't very happy about finding it on his property, and he knew exactly where to look for the culprit who built it."

My mother seemed to beam with glory, as if she alone cracked a mystery that nobody could solve. My heart sank; I suddenly felt as if I had been kicked in the stomach. *That* I could have handled, losing the cabin was the *coup de grace* of all debacles. I was shattered. My mother looked over her prey, like a vulture waiting patiently to pick at the bones.

When the cop had showed up at my parents' door, my mother was at first perplexed, claiming that I couldn't have built the cabin because I was in school. There was proof—incriminating evidence. Someone had left a smoky fire going in the stove. The neighbour picked up the telltale odour and followed it to the source. He was outraged. The cop, however, was thoroughly impressed with the amount of labour that went into it, and the intricate detail of the woodwork. That was little consolation to me. Perfunctory about my efforts, my father could hardly contain his anger. And although I removed only the wood stove, I left everything intact and never went back. Thirty-seven years later I made a pilgrimage to the site of my first cabin, parking my truck at the side of the Stouffville Side Road, knowing exactly where to go. The excavation was still there. Some ninety metres (one hundred yards) away was a newly constructed brick mansion with facades of cut limestone. The roof of my cabin had collapsed, of course the logs long ago rotted—mostly because I had left the bark on; the hemlock surrounding the site had grown proportionately, majestically, and no children had ever again walked the trails nearby, like we did then, the pathways clogged with deadfall, forest detritus and new growth. I pulled a rusted spike from one of the log ends protruding out of the ground and slipped it in my pocket. It all looked natural—the earth was claiming back this little bit of human effort—a portion of my history, long ago, it seemed.

May 1970.

Christ it was cold! It was snowing. Water splashed up the paddle shaft and froze, making it hard to get a firm grip without slipping. It was difficult keeping the canoe in a straight line, let alone catch up to the other canoe. I was paddling solo. Soren and Anders were up ahead, having their own problems by the look of things. I caught up.

"Let's get ashore," Soren yelled, "It's too windy!" It was also getting dark.

We pulled in to the lee of a large island, somewhere in the core archipelago of islands in Lake Temagami, and landed at a small beach. There was just enough room to pitch our tent, and pile rocks in a semi-circle for a crude fireplace in which to cook our rice and beans. An hour later, we were warmed,

fed and happy, staring contently into the devouring incandescence of the fire, consumed entirely by silence induced by fatigue and the mesmerizing flicker of orange flame.

Without a sound, a man stepped suddenly into the patina of fire-glow. He had a grizzled, expressionless face and was carrying an axe and he just stood there, staring, saying nothing. We were afraid to move. The large man started to laugh, which did nothing to purge our fear.

"Ah rest up lads, I'm just trying to get yer goat," the man beamed. "I'm Peter Norby—the Swede—I live over in the bay, right over there." He pointed, but we saw no lights in that direction. He put his axe down. "I was wonderin' who was camped here, so early in the spring—the ice's just off the lake yesterday, ya knows that I guess do ya?" We said we didn't and that we were just canoeing through, heading up to the Lady Evelyn River.

"Pretty place I hear, but I never been up there—rough too—geezly portages, been here most of my life," Norby informed us. We started to relax, ask him questions about what he did, about Temagami. He told us to come over in the morning to see his cabin. Norby apologized for scaring us and left as quietly as he had appeared. The next morning, after oatmeal and raisins, we bushwhacked to Norby's cabin. He was outside stuffing clothes into an open oil drum that had been filled with water and propped up on a rock firepit.

"It's washin' day, boys, once a year," and he stirred the steaming pot like a Shakespearian witch from *Macbeth*. We avoided the effluent, standing upwind from the flume of vaporous malodour. "When the clothes are done I climbs in and have me yearly bath," Norby explained, but we weren't going to stick around for that particular cleansing ceremony.

It turned out that Peter Norby had worked for the local Hudson's Bay Company factor as a cabin builder. *That* perked my attention. He travelled Lake Temagami in a big raft, big enough to carry a Belgian workhorse that he used to haul logs out of the bush with. And, as the walls of the cabin went up, the horse was used to lever the logs into place along the higher rounds. His own cabin was the old horse stable, redefined and modified only slightly to accommodate a personal euphoria only a modestly psychotic recluse might enjoy. We listened to story after story, enthralled, captured by this old man's charm and gift of gab. The morning was disappearing fast and the wind had rekindled some of its spring vibrancy. Not wild enough, though, to dissuade three impassioned youths from climbing into their canoes and striking off against the waves.

Four months earlier that year, while in the firm clutch of winter, restless beyond all reckoning, the three of us huddled around a kitchen table, dipping strips of Wonder Bread into our respective saucers filled with Crown corn syrup, listening intently to the man who would change the course of our lives.

Frank McConnaghy was our High School math teacher, and a very poor one at that. He was as enthusiastic about teaching us math as we were in learning it. What he did notice, at least in Soren and me, was that thousand-mile stare out the classroom window—a look we exercised often: a gleam in our eyes—a wanderlust that displaced any common denominator that, in some way, might prejudice the "Adventure." McConnaghy took our little coterie of misfits in as his own boys, feeding us stories about his own woodland travels, of having actually met the infamous Grey Owl in the 1920s, about this wonderful place called Temagami.

"Who was Grey Owl? Where is Temagami?" We peppered McConnaghy with endless questions, hungry to learn more. We wanted to go beyond paddling Algonquin Park with its tended trails; Temagami had a magic ring to it—a wildness that remained inviolate and untrammelled. McConnaghy was more than willing to share what he knew. A sadly beautiful man, then in his late fifties, living alone with his German Sheppard dog Buck, he had never remarried after his wife and children were all killed in a tragic car-train collision that had happened years before. His personal grief was never obvious to us, except perhaps in his deeply-set eyes; and he was careful not to show us slides or pictures of his family while we were there, choosing to remain aloof from his own world of melancholy.

"Read these," McConnaghy said, handing us copies of Grey Owl's *Men of the Last Frontier* and *Tales of an Empty Cabin,* and Henry David Thoreau's *Walden.* Sticky saucers were cleared and an old, tattered map showing Temagami was spread out over the table. "Grey Owl Country," he remarked, sweeping his hand in a broad arc across the map. Indian names tagged the numerous lakes, reading like a Longfellow poem: *Wawiagama, Wasaksina, Obabika, Wakimika, Temagami*—the magic unveiled itself. We were drawn in like trout to a fly, and reeled in hook-line-and-sinker.

"It's much wilder than Algonquin," McConnaghy assured us, not that we really had to be convinced. Temagami appeared as a panacea to end an increasingly prosaic school life. Soren would get the map copied and we would depart in early May; loss of school time was not even a consideration. Grey Owl's woodland narratives and Thoreau's contempt for the *desperate society,* modelled our consciousness of thought, making it all the more difficult to drift into the mainstream.

We bucked a steady headwind straight out of the wild northwest. Several times over the next two days we were forced to lay up during the day, huddled by a fire, and paddle in the evening when the cold wind had calmed. Sleeping in the open, we were vulnerable to random "attacks" by snowshoe hare, those crazed rabbits that found pleasure in running across our sleeping bags and chewing the leather straps fastened to our Deluth packs—including the leather belt that hoisted up my drawers! Anders had even complained about hares biting his feet through his sleeping bag. *If the rabbits are this vicious, Lord knows how dangerous the bears might be!*

At a gull rookery in the middle of Obabika Lake, we stopped to pick up several gull eggs to cook for breakfast. This turned out to be a bad idea. The eggs did not coagulate like ordinary eggs when cooked, and the fishy smell was so hideous that we abandoned breakfast altogether. For another two days we edged slowly northwards, wending our way up the Wakimika River, through ancient cedar forests and boreal swamps lined with marsh marigold and pitcher plants. A storm struck so violently and without warning that we barely had enough time to set up a rain tarp on a rock terrace on Wakimika Lake. We waited another day for the weather to calm itself. As it turned out, several tornadoes had ripped across the frontier lands north of Sudbury, not far from where we had camped that night in Temagami.

We arrived at a ghost town about the time we were ready for a good respite from weather and wind. It was an old lumber camp, circa 1950s, nestled quietly in the confines of a rocky bluff near the west end of Diamond Lake. It was one of Jim Murphy's camps—a major depot, replete with dining hall and cookhouse, bunkies, blacksmith shop, stable and five-seater kybo. Most of the buildings were hastily constructed from rough lumber, milled at the site and then sheathed in layers of heavy tarpaper; three log cabins were remarkably well preserved, although woodchucks had moved in to claim some of the woodwork as part of their territory, along with a plethora of snakes, voles, mice and other vermin. The location was stunning. The camp sat on a low, sand flat below the thirty-metre (about one-hundred-foot) cliff, rimmed by three-hundred-year-old red and white pine trees—the *arbor vitae* of Ontario. There were at least a dozen shacks, sheds and cabins, most of which were already fallen or under duress from the elements and heavy snows. Scattered about were remnant wooden boats, archaic snow-cats, dismembered vehicles and a great number of horse-drawn sledges, lined up against each other creating a moiré effect. Twenty years of new growth, mostly paper birch and aspen, had pushed up through camp detritus like garden sculptures; birdsong and the chatterings of woodchucks and red squirrels augured the notion that the ghost town had merely changed hands and was actually no ghost town at all.

Fishing for pike proved to be exceptional, right off the shore in front of the main cabin; in fact, the cabin was so inviting (and free of blackflies) we elected to stay over a couple days to catch our breath. The pike was barbecued over an open fire in front of our new boothy. The cabin was in good shape, save for a few leaks in the roof, and a stove that had seen better days. Once the sun set, the deer mice transmogrified an inanimate structure into a veritable living insane asylum. They were everywhere. And trying to sleep was an exercise of futility, having to constantly brush them off our sleeping bags or wake up with one still clinging to an earlobe or finger was nothing short of discomfiting. I was getting a good dose of cabin modality, annoying yes, but resident mice were no more irksome than blackflies on the outside—all part and parcel of the wilderness lifestyle on the trail. Nobody dared to complain.

The next morning Soren and I sat on the grass in front of the cabin while Anders puttered around the camp looking for artifacts. Now that my friend Ed had had found girls to be of more interest than outdoor pursuits, Soren and I had kindled a stalwart friendship dedicated to unmitigated freedom. Certainly not to be constrained by silly emotional frivolities such as dating, we now talked of making a pledge to spend a whole year living in the wild, to build our own cabin in the woods. The seed was planted. At our feet, a

large garter snake edged along, moving slowly in the frost-rimed grass; about eight inches from its tail, I noticed a large portion of its flesh was missing, like a huge bite. Darting in and out of cover was a shrew. Taking advantage of the snake's lethargy, the shrew would run up and tear chunks of flesh from the snake that was unable to defend itself in the cold. Neither Soren nor I intervened, but, instead, watched with curiosity at one of Nature's cruel realities. Like the snake, I felt that society was constantly chewing away at my soul, making too many demands; out here everything made sense, at least the shrew needed to eat, and the snake was foolish enough not to find shelter beneath the cabin. Each knew its place in the general scheme of things. You make mistakes—Nature makes the appropriate selection as to who will survive. I liked that credo. It was straightforward, understandable, simple—no hidden agendas, no profit mongering and no ladders to climb. If you fell out here, you just get back up and start all over again at the same level—that is, if you were able to get up at all.

It was hard to leave the sanctuary of the cabin, mice *et al*; but beyond the "creature" comforts the adventure still beckoned. As we charted our course north towards Maple Mountain, the weather turned from balmy to blizzard in a matter of a few hours, typical for the month of May when the world is still much closer to winter than it is to summer. Brisk northwest winds spirited through the valleys, carrying with it the notion that spring did not intend to settle in just yet. The Lady Evelyn River lay ahead of us like an insurmountable staircase; snow threatened and the rocks on the shore landings and along bony portage trails began to ice over in the freezing rain. But beyond the obvious travails, the river remained provocative and beautifully sculpted and displayed in its entire post-winter drabness, leaden granite and olive forest backdrop floating between black water and silver-bearded sky, aloof, uninviting in its damp trappings and sodden woods. The worse the weather turned, the more we felt as if we were incongruous with the land around us, vulnerable and unprepared. We moved cautiously upstream, past the first falls—a short carry, deceptively easy—then on to the next portage around Center Falls. We learned that the regal Lady beheld not only an aesthetical appeal but could easily turn on you in fits of foreboding countenance, demanding, moody and treacherous. By all measures of time and circumstance, we were the first to explore the river, as it seemed, having been lured in to the depths of Temagami as mere boys, chaste and untested; certainly no one person could have braved such indomitable wilderness before us. The portages remained unmarked, except for occasional rock cairns and old axe blazes on the trees, suggesting that no park rangers existed in these parts, charged with the duty of posting signs telling us where to unload, where to camp, where to shit. Center Falls, colloquially known as "The Golden Staircase," proved to be a demanding carry—almost a kilometre of terraced bedrock over which one is required to step up constantly, farther than is biophysically possible to do so under duress of load. Helen Falls portage was even more tenuous, having to scramble over loose shale, vertically to a plateau of glaciated fissures and tumbled scree, glued together by bottomless sinkholes of bog. Hours later, we had not yet reached Divide Lake. Instead of portaging up into the lake, we opted for a short cut, cross-country, to the south channel where we were heading anyway. This proved to be a fiasco. In the North Country, there is no such thing as a short cut. Tired beyond all sensibility, soaked from sweat and wet snow, we collapsed by the river's edge in a confused heap with no place to camp amongst the slabs of granite. To add injury to insult, I had split my lip open while collecting firewood. We had definitely entered an entirely unforgiving and relentless wilderness. In youthful arrogance, I maintained a combative, spiritually deprived stand against Nature. I was not going to be overwhelmed.

I was in "survival" mode, as were the others, inviolable and self-important; but it had not dawned on me that this might be the reason why we were not faring so well under present conditions. The three of us crammed into the small, nylon emergency tent and slept. Our frigid sarcophagus, by morning, had all but collapsed under the weight of heavy snow. Everything wet from the day before had frozen solid overnight: boots, gloves, discarded watersoaked underclothing resembled bricks until thoroughly heated by the morning fire. On these premier sojourns, extra articles of clothing or boots were considered extraneous luxuries we could do without. Keeping things dry was an art yet to be perfected. That we had a tent at all was unusual. The noble Lady flowed by our sorry camp, pregnant with wintermelt.

The sun attempted to part the grey pall and import a friendlier embrace, like a warm blanket draped over the monochromatic landscape. The snow melted quickly, but the rocks along the portage remained slippery with the patina of winter mold and wet snow—the shadowy world of the trail, reluctant to open its dense canopy to the morning brilliance.

Approaching the first falls, we could smell wood smoke. *Out here, now, how could that be?* I mused, almost disappointed that there might be another soul in *our* wilderness, camped up ahead. There was a single canoe pulled up on shore, just right of the cataracts marking the fall. As we pushed on, our map proved to be next to worthless at marking the location of portage trails; exacting a location to unload and carry was done simply by quick deduction; anything obvious, like an overturned canoe, signalled a call to pull over and investigate. The portage was rough enough, and after ninety metres (about a hundred yards), we were forced to disengage our loads at a break in the Jack pines that lined the "trail." We stood at a long, sloping bedrock terrace; before us, riverside, was a neatly trimmed, brown log cabin, and set below the cabin, overlooking the falls, was a quaint canopied gazebo. An elderly man was waving us over.

Excited to know more about this haven in the midst of rock and pine, miles from anywhere, we complied and met the man on the deck with a barrage of questions. He welcomed us by pouring freshly brewed coffee in real ceramic mugs. "They're from my brothers' restaurant in Fredonia, New York—a nice luxury out here," the man explained with an air of pardonable pride. He punched a double hole in a tin of evaporated milk and pushed it our way. The three of us looked at each other and telepathically exchanged the word *milk?*

"Here, have some sugar. You boys seem to need it right about now." We spooned sugar into our cups until they overflowed.

He introduced himself as Dick Lathrop, and he had come up early on his own to open up the camp; his brother Max was ill and nobody else could make the trip. Dick had flown in from Temagami a couple of days earlier but had had some difficulty getting downriver from Divide Lake, the water being so high and the portage trails flooded. We were given a brief history of the cabin, built forty years ago by a Cleveland lawyer. Lathrop himself was getting on in years, in his sixties, overweight, and extremely cordial. I liked him immediately and I felt that the feeling was mutual.

Saddened by his inability to carry any significant load over the portages, let alone a heavy canvas canoe, and the difficulty of coercing any member of his fraternity (the Dirty Dozen Club) to make the pilgrimage to Cabin Falls, Lathrop shared his trepidations about the general upkeep of the camp. Looking around, I noticed the quickly deteriorating condition of the cabin, the plank walkways and the gazebo. Being the eternal optimist, I offered to take care of it for him in exchange for the use of the cabin on future trips to Temagami, which by now was a certainty in my mind. Lathrop was overjoyed with the proposition. Scribbling down his address on the back of a cigarette box, he muttered something about paying for materials to replace the roofing and the flight to fly them in. We set a tentative date for late fall. Soren would be in university, but Anders could take the time off to go with me.

Finally, we were warming up, and it was not easy to tear ourselves away from these luxuries—the hot coffee, the setting, our congenial host who made it difficult for us to get on our way by offering biscuits and coffee refills. We all relaxed into the omnipresent din of the falls, voices raised a pitch to rise above the cacophony of water tumbling through the chasm.

When we did part, I felt that I would, someday, become conjoined with this wonderful place at the falls; call it a premonition or gut feeling, the seed was planted for a new adventure that was sure to unfold sometime in the future. The Lady Evelyn River was seeping into my bloodstream like an organic elixir: the moist breath of her waterfalls, the swirling eddies intricately laced with white foam, the abruptness of the canyons, the exuberant aroma of pine, the sweet taste of the water—an endless assault on the senses. *This felt like home to me—this stark boldness and natural chaos that expounded a profound purpose, complex and confrontational.* I was becoming part of this bold landscape in no small way. I felt safe here, welcomed, comforted in a natural, innate, serendipitous milieu. There were no boundaries here, only the trail through the wilderness and the freedom to do what I pleased, without judgment or prejudice.

This premier Temagami voyage brought my life into clear perspective. Having just finished high school, certainly not as an exemplary student, I had turned down a rather lucrative job as a catalogue artist for a major Toronto department store. The rationale behind that decision, much to the chagrin of my parents, was simple—I did not want anything to jeopardize my liberty to paddle. Had I accepted the city job, my life would have unfolded in a disparately different manner; money meant little to me if I were to compromise that freedom. The metamorphosis taking place in my soul also revealed how precarious and brittle my home life had become. World politics continued to excrete a madness that left everyone edgy and paranoid. Canoeing in the wilderness with a dream of owning my own cabin became my mantra.

As our canoe trip progressed, Maple Mountain and the Lady Evelyn wilderness faded into the background. The Montreal River, *moni-ang-zibi,* absorbed the outflow of the Lady Evelyn into its murky embrace. The Montreal had been dammed along its upper course but the lower river, according to our less than reliable map, meandered haphazardly but perceivably pristine to the Ottawa River—our objective, to be followed by a cruise down the Ottawa as far as the town of Mattawa. We were about to be shaken out of our illusions of utopia by the sad realities of an economic boom.

The river flowed inviolate, but the land that defined the Montreal had been denuded of all timber, right to the very shoreline. All that remained were the stubs of saplings and stumps of magnificent pine trees, for as far as the eye could wander. *What was happening?* There was no sight of anyone around. The river valley had been skinned clean to the bone. The viscera of a deer lay strung along a vague portage trail, the animal having been disembowelled by one of the sharp "pungy" sticks left behind after being cut by a brushing axe. No birds sang. Even the voice of the rapids was strained through clenched teeth. Without the forest to hold back the meltwater, flow had diminished quickly, leaving a pallid, exsanguinated river full of white boulders. Lining and wading with the canoes became treacherous. I had lost my running shoes in one of the rapids and was now forced to portage in bare feet. We slept that night in a sawyer's tent, found unoccupied, standing like a tombstone in a wasted netherworld of slash and carnage.

The following day, rounding a bend, we practically canoed into a sign strung across the river, "*Do not proceed past this point—river ahead channeled into inflow culverts.*" The river had ended. There was no place to go. A truck went by on the ridge above the river. A new road. Hauling our gear and canoes up through the tangle of detritus left behind by the work gangs, we dumped everything on the roadside and waited for another truck. Within minutes, a truck stopped and the driver was more than willing to drive us the three miles to the Ottawa River. We sat in the back of the truck holding the canoes down while bouncing along the gravel road. Like an anthill that had been ripped apart, huge excavations swarming with earthmovers loomed beside us. The contrast between this place and the Lady Evelyn was shocking.

"We're building the Lower Notch hydro dam," the hard-hatted driver yelled out proudly from the driver's seat. None of us felt like talking. Upon reaching the Ottawa River, we thanked the man for the ride and made a quick attempt to quell the sick feeling in our stomachs by getting canoe bound. This did assuage the nausea, and I noticed we were paddling quite hard in order to dispel the resident gloom. Our world now green and full again, the wide river carrying us along, our adventure continued but not without a residue of aggravation at having been witness to such wanton destruction. *"Dona Naturae Pro Populo Sunt"*—the gifts of nature are for the people—so goes the Ontario Hydro motto. Wilderness had been "de-natured" and packaged just so someone in Toronto, or Ottawa, could run their juice blender.

In a way, the contraposition of wilderness versus industrial progress became a revelation to me. It was an awakening to the state of affairs shaping (or misshaping) the Canadian hinterlands. And since I preferred knowing in terms of clarity, those distinctions that govern over our general well-being, *my* beloved wilderness direly needed the services of a crusader. But I knew nothing about environmental crusading. In 1970, there was virtually no environmental movement in Canada—or the world for that matter. The Vancouver, British Columbia-based "Don't Make a Wave Committee," a small group of pot-crazed hippies opposing nuclear weapons testing by the United States, wouldn't formalize their new group, Greenpeace, until 1971. Its first president would be long-haired columnist for the *Vancouver Sun*, Bob Hunter, who, oddly enough, twenty years later would become one of my most trusted compatriots and warrior brothers.

Once this flagship canoe trip to Temagami was over, I began planning the next one.

Much had happened through the summer. My father had suffered a severe stroke the year before and never quite recovered, and by early fall my parents divorced and the family home was sold. My brother and sister went their own respective ways, and I moved in to an old chicken shed that I had renovated, some distance north of Toronto. I should have been distressed about the outcome; instead, I was relieved because the slow demise of our family was now over.

I had time to concentrate on my artwork and had secured tidy little contracts with the Austin-Marshal Card Company, Simpson's Department Store, the Pioneer Village and Armadale Communications. Pen-and-ink renderings were still considered chic, especially in the advertising circles, and I did well, made the right contacts, and worked only when I wasn't canoeing or touring on my motorcycle. I would work diligently on commission pieces until they were done, make just enough money to grubstake another canoe trip (groceries for a month would cost about forty dollars), and then head north, usually to various points in Temagami, or cycling in Quebec.

I also couldn't get the little cabin on the falls out of my mind. It was such an alluring place—a castle in the wilderness. Lathrop had bought a new stove and tarpaper for the roof and left it at Lakeland Airways, ready for when Anders and I had the time to do the work. The season was just about over and the smaller lakes had already started to freeze over, but by the second week of November, Bob Gareh, chief pilot and owner of the air service, told us that if we didn't fly in now, we weren't "bloody well going to!"

I had to get up there—one more time before the year was out; luckily, Anders was free for time so we quickly packed for cold weather and left for Temagami. We flew in the Cessna 180, two trips, one for us and the canoe—the other to haul in two rolls of heavy tarpaper, a new wood stove and pipe, and miscellaneous gear. It was a rough flight, windy, but at least the rain had let up and there was no snow on the ground yet. Darkness set in quickly. Leaving all but the required night gear behind at the landing, we paddled downriver to the cabin. I had to line the canoe down the rapids because of the low water, usually not a difficult task today, but back then "lining" meant that you had to actually wade in the river up to your groin to work the canoe through the rocks. The water was frigid, and by the time we reached the cabin and ignited a fire, I was mildly hypothermic.

For the next several days, the temperature barely rose above freezing, and the job of patching the roof became a painstakingly laborious job. But between bouts of cold, rain and cabin work I was enjoying the routine of cabin living immensely, frying bannocks, building bunks, playing cribbage by candlelight. We had decided to take down the rafters holding up the rat's nest of cabin detritus, and give the place some breathing room. Aside from the moldy sleeping bags, mouse turds and superfluous, useless junk, we found a few treasures. One was a Remington, model 41-P, Targetmaster, bolt-action, single shot .22 calibre rifle with leather sling (but no bullets); the other was a Roxy Victrola, replete with a stack of 78 rpm records, some cut as early as 1905. The Roxy was frayed and tattered at the edges with damp-rusted, buckle-down fasteners, a burn mark from being set too close to a gas lantern, or someone leaving a cigarette propped on it, and the ill-fitting sound piece was snugged on to the swing arm with a piece of yellow cardboard coil. If you let the playing arm run to the end of a record, it would suddenly fly across the disc and send the sound piece hurling to the floor. The turntable did not run level, playing havoc with the needle. The records were scratchy and stained, probably from something sticky spilled on them and left to dry while stacked. But the sound of Leo Reisman and His Orchestra playing Oscar Hammerstein's, "Why Was I Born," from the musical comedy *Sweet Adeline,* drifted hauntingly throughout the tiny cabin, as if Robert Newcomb had just arrived for a party. Anders and I went through the stack of records: Bud Cooper and Sammy Stept singing "I Care for Her and She Cares for Me," in a 1920s canned megaphonic style; Jack Smith—the whispering Baritone; a comedy sketch by Moran and Mock called "Two Black Crows;" Teddy Ralph singing "When I Take My Sugar to Tea." All were tantamount to the most exemplary entertainment.

We were pushing the season to its outer edge, knowing well that we should have paddled out earlier. But it was hard to leave the euphoric pleasures of cabin life, regardless of the snow that began to fall and the ice that was now forming along the shallow rim of shoreline where the current was negligible. It was the middle of November.

I had dreamed that night that the canoe had overturned on Lake Temagami, and I saw myself gripping the side of the canoe with waning strength as my life was being sapped by the cold water. It was unnerving. I didn't share this with Anders. He was entirely cerebral and practical, and a devout spiritual iconoclast; conversations over the past week, if they happened at all, were brief and pragmatic. He was, though, good ballast in the canoe. The dream was my own secret calamity.

Downriver travel from the cabin was not easy; the cold and snow left a slick rime over everything, and getting the canoe through the rapids demanded utmost attention to staying as dry as possible—an almost futile expectation. The three-plus-kilometre (two-mile) portage into Diamond Lake lived up to its name as the "Dead Man's March," although we were much warmer

walking than paddling. We were so stiff and cold, that by the time we reached the north end of Lake Temagami, we had to pull up and walk about to get the circulation back in our feet. The lake was rough, whitecapping, and the shore splash turned quickly to ice, making it difficult to beach the canoe. We elected to land at a summer campsite in the narrows before entering the main body of Lake Temagami, pulled up the canoe and walked to the nearby cover of trees for warmth out of the wind. The canoe slipped silently off the shore and floated away.

When we saw the canoe out in the bay, drifting in the wind out to the main flow of the lake and waves, the only thing we could do was curse. Everything we owned was in the canoe; there were no boats and certainly no float planes about this time of the season. Life jackets were rarely worn and usually shoved under the canoe seats. Immediately I realized there was only one thing to do and that was to swim out to the canoe. I barely had time to remove my heavy boots, let alone anything else, and plunged into the lake, disregarding the freezing water. I felt myself go deep but managed to keep my head above the water. Moving out fast, before my clothes became lead weights, I swam awkwardly to the canoe. It seemed farther away than I had thought, or maybe had been carried further out by the wind, but I could now feel the numbness setting in to my lower extremities. I put my hands on the gunnels and pulled myself in to the boat, yelling to Anders to get a fire going. Anders had the uncanny knack of killing a fire with wet wood, or taking an inordinately long time to ignite one; what was worse was that we were at a heavily used campsite where firewood was scarce. When I reached shore and secured our canoe, I stripped down to my underwear and stood barefoot in the snow, jumping around to ward off a chill. Anders' first attempt at making a fire failed. I ran shoeless in the snow, scrounging birchbark and cedar sprigs until I had enough tinder to get a fire going. It took a while in the wind, but it burned vigorously enough to buy some time to gather what wood we could find. The wind was numbing; it also made the fire burn far too quickly for the amount of wood we gleaned from the site. I wrapped myself in a Hudson's Bay wool blanket while we collected enough dry clothing out of our duffel bag. The dry clothes felt good and I praised myself for taking off my boots. The wet clothing took two hours to dry over the fire before we could get going again. And to this day, as I remember well the ferocity of the lake, the breaking white waves, and the tiny wood craft we were paddling. Why we didn't perish that November was a phenomenon.

That event did nothing to bring me closer to understanding the limitations of my passion for adventure; in fact, if anything, it made me all the more defiant, regardless of consequences, believing that nothing could diminish my quest for independence. In my youthful arrogance, I manufactured an inflexible "cause and effect" attitude to almost every facet of my life; the world was fucked up, my parents were fucked up, so I felt the need to fight back against the system in order to effect some semblance of order in an otherwise chaotic life. Balance—a Libran cachet. I was struggling to believe in something tangible; religion with a spiteful God at the helm did not quite play out the role model I was hoping for, and I was too self-absorbed in my own headspace to evolve to a higher consciousness. Spirituality, in an organic, earthly sense, was elusive. I pushed myself physically in order to experience some sort of esoteric ordinance that complied with a narrow view of reality. And it would be some time before that door to personal enlightenment would open.

Seven: Winter on Diamond Lake

Every mile is two in winter.
George Herbert, 1593-1633

When I woke up there was half-a-foot of snow over my sleeping bag. The wind had blown so fiercely through the night that snow had funnelled into a small opening in my canvas bivouac and settled in a drift over my bed. Still in my bag, I lit the trail stove, having set aside enough firewood to kindle a morning fire. The chill dissipated quickly and I put on a pot of water for an oatmeal breakfast. I poked my head outside and was buffeted by a steady wind and blowing snow, so thick that I could barely make out my toboggan leaning against a tree only a few feet away. A great deal of snow had already fallen during the night and there was no sign that the weather would change anytime soon.

The Diamond Lake cabin was at least six miles away to the west. Soren was there, along with his two brothers who had flown in by ski plane a few days back. It felt crowded with the four of us in the cabin so I had packed up my toboggan, the canvas tarps and trail stove, enough food for three days and trekked off on a solo venture. The weather had proven to be fair, cold and the snowpack conducive to fair travelling. But I had seen a remarkable sun dog yesterday, on a clear and sunny afternoon, and knew well enough that my luck with the weather wouldn't hold. I had followed a small chain of lakes north off Diamond, found a lovely place to pitch my camp, and explored in relative bliss and solitude. Now, I had to make a judgment call—to stay put and wait out the blizzard (which may take two to three days), or to try and make it back to the cabin before the return trip became too difficult in the deep snow.

Reluctantly, I chose to break camp, pack up and leave my little sanctuary. That was an almost costly mistake. The wet snow made it toilsome; I had to stop every six metres (twenty feet) to clear the snow buildup on the toboggan and knock the wadded ice off the bottom of my snowshoes. I could still make out the depression left by my old snowshoe track; it was harder packed than the soft snow around it, so I tried to follow it back out to Diamond Lake. There was a brief respite from the storm amongst the trees separating the two lakes and progress was slow but appreciably easy. Once I reached the expanse of Diamond, it was another story altogether. My original hard-packed trail had disappeared entirely; still, I tried to follow it by maintaining a "proceed by feel" method—when my snowshoes slipped off the trail and sank into the deepening slush I would sometimes have to get down on my hands and knees to try and feel for it with my hands. Sometimes the toboggan would slip off the trail and mire in the wet snow, and the slush would freeze to the bottom. I would then flip over the loaded toboggan and scrape the ice off with my sheath knife. This went on endlessly.

The packed lake trail went right down the middle of the lake—just like neophyte summer paddlers. That put the shoreline on either side of me at least half a mile or more away. I had lost all reference points in the blizzard. My world was an enveloping white one, profoundly disorienting, lonely. All I could do was to keep the wind at my back. And it was an obstinate wind, fierce with energy, chilling the air with its bleak momentum, yet, oddly helping to push me along, inching forward with interminably languorous progress.

I took off my parka to keep from overheating, but doing this exposed the back of my neck to the wind. The chilling effect and the quick cooling of bloodlines to my brain made me a little stupid. I was losing it. I was in trouble. Energy spent, no immediate shelter, and with still over five kilometres (three miles) of heavy going to get to the cabin, I began second-guessing my intuition. I wanted to rest, lie down and maybe sleep awhile—it would have been so easy, comforting—*suicidal.* I tried to remain lucid, to concentrate on moving forward. *Focus, dammit, focus!* I kept saying to myself there was a warm cabin at the end of all this.

The blizzard worsened, if that was possible, and it was hard to stand up without the support of the track line to the toboggan pulled tautly around my shoulder. With the deepening snow, the old trail was impossible to follow. I just gave up and resolved to plunge ahead, no matter what.

Three months earlier, when the comet Kahoutek careened across the firmament, and soothsayers were predicting all manner of miracles and catastrophes, I lay in a hospital bed recovering from a burst appendix. The first doctor I had consulted told me it was a simple "belly ailment" and I was to go home and sleep it off—the pain would subside; this precocious diagnosis, I presumed, was prompted due to my not owning hospital insurance. *Another facet of a feckless system to be mistrusted,* I thought. I was brushed off. I was staying with friends at the time, and when they discovered me lying on the floor, unable to move, ashen complexion whiter than hoarfrost and eyes sinking into my skull, I was rushed to emergency where I was quickly operated on. The operation would have cost over eight hundred dollars, adding a hundred each day I stayed in the hospital, but the doctor was sympathetic and allowed me to backdate my insurance and I was let out of the hospital in less than a week—a week earlier than normal.

In a way, Kahoutek may have been my salvation. I was to have embarked on a long winter trek with Soren, bound for the Diamond Lake cabin, only days after the comet made its brief appearance. Had my appendix burst while out in the wilderness, isolated some 65 kilometres (40 miles) from the nearest town, I may have certainly died. The trip was postponed, but only briefly, long enough to collect my gear, purchase supplies for two months or more, and buy train tickets to Temagami. I had only been out of the hospital for a paltry few days; my incisions hadn't healed and I was extremely weak. But I was determined, and Soren mused that he would look after me. Instead of feeling vulnerable, I maintained a stoic, almost deathless temperament. The year before, while winter camping with Anders in Algonquin Park, I froze the ends off two toes because I had tightly buckled frozen boots into my snowshoe harnesses. Three days in the hospital and two months of rehabilitation, the excruciating pain taught me little. Angry at my weakness, I hobbled out from home to the nearby woods, axe in hand, intent on building a winter bivouac. In my awkwardness, I put the axe through the toe of my good foot. Limping home on two injured feet, a trail of blood signaturing the snow, my winter escapades were over for the year.

When the opportunity arose to spend the winter on Diamond Lake, Soren and I were ecstatic. The operation did not dampen my enthusiasm. But when we exited the train and began pulling our one-hundred-and-fifty-pound loaded toboggans across the deeply crusted lake snow, each jarring step tugged at the stitches in my belly. We had only trekked half a mile and I felt like I was going to bust a seam. Soren, who was breaking trail, came back to where I was sitting hunched over my load—he was worried but compassionate.

"Let's fly in, it's the only way," I said, pointing to the two planes in front of the air service hangar. They were both on skis. Soren complied, knowing that was our only option other than going back home.

Bob Gareh agreed to fly us in the Cessna 180 and the Piper Cub for forty-two dollars. "You boys are crazy, you won't last two weeks!" Gareh resounded with an air of officiousness. He took our money quickly before we had a chance to change our minds about the trip. Gareh was the second person that day to tell us that; earlier, at the local coffee shop, the Busy Bee, we were approached by the district game warden, who shall be nameless, who made no bones about representing the Queen's business, stating that we were not allowed to camp more than twenty-one days in one location on Crown Land. We told him that we had planned to move around a lot over the winter. Still, the warden eyed us with suspicion, as if we were intending on trapping or hunting illegally. We each had a .22 calibre rifle packed in our duffel, out of sight; with our plans to hunt small game and set up a snare line for rabbits, the guns would come in handy.

There was no heat in the Piper Cub, but this discomfort slipped quickly into unconscious thought as the landscape rolled by, a thousand feet below me—sixty-five kilometres (forty miles) of monochromatic wilderness I didn't have to plough through on snowshoes. The Diamond Lake cabin lay below, almost buried in winter vestment, visible only as a pronounced hummock of drifted snow. In a matter of minutes we had landed, disembowelled the plane of its contents, and watched with bated excitement as the pilots steered their planes back to town. Then it was silent.

Like a sponge soaking up water, winter snow absorbs sound like a great white vacuum. Sound was "felt" rather than heard, as short, sharp intrusions—the snap of a frozen tree on a sub-zero night, the boom of lake ice as it shifts its weight, the short retorts of bird calls, the crunching of snow underfoot. Our own voices cut the air with sharp, icy edges—words covered in hoarfrost. So different from travelling spring to fall when sounds invade the wilderness from all directions, without hiatus, dominated by evening cricket and echoing loon through the "quiet" hours of darkness, erupting at dawn to a medley of forest voices and the sound of water lapping the shore or tumbling over rapids. In winter, there is only the all-encompassing silence. And if you don't assimilate quickly to its nuance, the mind resolves to inform you that your apprehensions are well founded and you have no right to be where you are. This was the very first time I had accepted any of Nature's immutable secrets—the preciousness of silence as a commodity—defined acutely by the clash and clangour of city street and the unrefined surge of human intercourse. I had become so accustomed to noise that silence, in its purest sense, became a luxury to me. Even winter camping in Algonquin Park with tent pitched miles from the nearest highway, the sound of trucks breaking and gearing resounded through the

night, constantly reminding me that I wasn't really that far from anything, and the wilderness I had elected to visit was merely a facade.

The initial two weeks at the cabin was hard for me. I was wrought with fatigue and I did little to help while Soren cut firewood and made the cabin livable. Bunks were built and the back end of the cabin was closed off so that we could conserve more firewood by living in a more heat-worthy environment. I spent most of my time writing in my diary and taking short snowshoe hikes from the cabin. I was gaining my strength back and excursions soon became longer, and chores were shared equally. There were always a surfeit of things to do, including: cutting firewood, keeping the water hole open of ice, setting and checking rabbit snares, packing trails and preparing meals. At least every week we ventured out for an overnight, exploring the lakes beyond the cabin, sometimes travelling ten or fifteen kilometres (six to nine miles). Sleeping in a makeshift lean-to, at first, was a cold affair having only a crude reflector-fire to keep us warm in a miserably inefficient way. The old lumber camp contained a wealth of discarded metal and I was fortunate to have found the right materials to fashion a trail stove out of a five-gallon steel pail, and stove pipe out of an old forge chimney vent. The stove and pipe could be packed easily onto a toboggan, and with two of our canvas tarps, a commendable shelter could be constructed. And it was put to good use when we left for a six-day-trek resupply to Bear Island. The trip was difficult, over new ground where trails had to be broken through tangled spruce and rockfall, following a long escarpment that eventually took us to Obabika Lake. There we hit a vicious snowstorm with blizzard-force winds, but the new heated bivouac proved its value by increasing our comfort zone tenfold.

At Bear Island we bought a few tin goods, treats and smoked bacon, mailed our letters and then stayed the night at the Petersen's on Garden Island, camping in one of the small sleep shacks used by summer staff of Camp Wabun. The next morning, Vagn Petersen gave us a lift up the lake by ski-doo to shorten the trip back to the cabin.

During the following two weeks, the temperature rarely rose above minus-thirty Celsius. These were halcyon days, regardless of the bitterness of the cold, and we settled in to a rhythm, enjoying each other's company and respecting our differences. Soren, the bird scientist, who later became Acadia University's ornithology professor, approached Nature in a secular way, with a strict adherence to modern, unidealistic scientific deduction. I, on the other hand, was the dreamer, the artist, always searching for an alternative answer for everything. Science, as far as I was concerned, was to blame for the sad state of world affairs. To Soren, birds sang in the spring because they were in pain caused by swollen gonads; I maintained the notion that birds sang merely because they were in love. Those differences between us eventually tested our patience to the outer limits. Having no other social intercourse but ourselves pushed the boundaries of friendship to the point of meltdown. Soren's two brothers flew in one day, bringing with them a paltry assortment of groceries, including one roadkill raccoon, which we immediately threw into a stew pot. After they showed no inclination to leave, and spoke amongst themselves in Danish, I was compelled to leave for a few days of solace.

Now, pushing through the oppressive drifts in a witless engagement of survival, I couldn't wait to see my insouciant friends. Long past the self-effacing criticism for not remaining where I was, I concentrated on putting one foot in front of the other, step by laborious step, legs moving on their own volition, keeping a direction towards where I thought the cabin was. The tumpline cut into my neck and shoulder, further restricting the circulation to my head and I was close to passing out. Realizing this, I stopped to re-adjust the line and put on my wool neckwarmer. It helped. I began seeing glimpses of trees between snow gusts, recognizing a point of land a mile from the cabin. I calculated that I had been travelling less than a mile an hour, and darkness with its sometimes inexorable punctuality, descended quickly over the non-landscape in ever-increasing dullness.

Warmth of a wood stove, the balsam smell of my bed, a warm cup of sweet Earl Grey tea, friends laughing—compelling luxuries enough to will more energy to press on. Finally, with a dim light from a lantern in the window, blurred but regular as a beacon on a sea coast, and the rim of trees on the cliff above the cabin were clearly visible, I now found the strength to reach my sanctuary. Utterly exhausted, I unpacked only my sleeping bag, entered the cabin to mild greetings, and slipped silently into my bunk.

Soren's brothers left by ski-plane shortly after and the adventure for us continued into March, through spring thaw and refreeze, which we took advantage of and walked the eighty kilometres (fifty miles) to the train station in Temagami, arriving at four in the morning, collapsing on the hard wooden benches and sleeping until the station master evicted us. Smelling of woodsmoke, dressed in greasy wool pants and torn sweaters, we drank coffee at the Busy Bee while the usual coterie of locals looked on disapprovingly. We both felt like weeping. The adventure was over. We were tired beyond recognition, but elated in having endured a most remarkable journey of discovery. And we realized that nobody would really understand what we had gone through, together, and alone on our own, without any connection to the outside world, and with miserly few possessions. Could we ever be as happy and at peace again? I believe that worried us both, that we would now get caught up in the mainstream and not be able to get out. Simplicity, just like Thoreau had taught us, to live deliberately and "suck the marrow out of life." And, like Thoreau, I suppose we left the woods for as good a reason as we went there.

Eight: Nitchee Keewense

*So I went on for some days cutting and hew-
ing timber, and also studs and rafters, all with
my narrow axe, not having many communica-
ble or scholar-like thoughts singing to myself.*
Henry David Thoreau, 1854

I was twenty-two years old when I met my second *real* Indian. My trepidations embodied all that I found distasteful in myself and in the culture that
had been assigned to me. I was white European, and probably in *his* eyes I
was as waspish as one could possibly be, in light of present circumstances. I
was *shaganash*—and with that expletive came the weight of four hundred
years of oppression against *his* People crashing down on my Imperialist head.
This was not the way it was supposed to happen! We were shaking hands, and
we suddenly became locked in a sort of cultural duel, and I'm sure that he
knew that my girlfriend was standing twenty feet behind us, shielded by a
huge pine tree, knife drawn for whatever purpose may have been demanded
of her to save me, or herself, from this savage. His hand was large, like a steel
vise, and I could feel the bones in my own hand yield slightly under the grasp
of which I could not escape until he decided to let go. He remained sitting in
his steel boat. I crouched by the shore. He said nothing but simply raised his
hand in a gesture of friendliness: the moment his hand surrounded mine it
was like stepping into a leg-hold animal trap. I surveyed his boat, noting that
the motor had no cowling over it, there was no life jacket anywhere, no oar
or paddle; an assortment of tools lay strewn about as if scattered ceremoni-
ously for decoration, and about four inches of ice water sloshed around his
Wellingtons. It was obvious he cared little for the Canadian safe-boating regu-
lations. His eyes scanned my campsite. A wry smile curled his lip, more in a
grimace than a friendly gesticulation. The vice squeezing my hand tightened.
"I could make fun of you," he said without expression. He looked again at my
camping accoutrement scattered amongst the tall pines. *Shit,* I thought, and I
knew exactly what he was looking at. "I could make fun of you…but I won't,"

he said again rather smartly, as if what he was looking at was typical of a white man in the wilderness.

In the middle of the campsite stood a Quebec heater—an upright wood stove—and I had fastened a couple of lengths of stovepipe on top to better direct the smoke from the fire that burned briskly inside. It did look pretty strange from his perspective—a canoeist travelling with a 200-pound wood stove. *But I couldn't tell him that the stove was for a cabin we were building—an illegal cabin at that, with the intention of squatting on the Queens' property (arguably Indian Land), and we had ignited the stove to conserve fuelwood (which made total sense to us).* Still, the whole scene looked rather absurd and I was to quietly suffer the indignation of being *shaganash* rather than betray our mission. We had now been shaking hands for about five minutes and I was afraid that when I withdrew my hand it would come out without any fingers attached.

"I'm Mack McKenzie," he told me. "Big M, they call me. What's your name?" Reluctantly I told him my name. "What kind of name is that?" he queried. "Ya mean like, Hap-hazard," he said jokingly. I tried to laugh, but a nervous lump in my throat thwarted any attempt of being even benignly sociable. Big M invited me to stop by his house on the reserve (and he motioned that my friend behind the tree with the knife was welcome too), and that he was the only Indian on the Bear Island that owned a colour TV. I nodded politely and he let go of my hand; the isostatic rebound of compressed bone and tissue painfully reshaping the fingers to their customary alignment.

As he left in his boat, crashing through what was left of the candling lake ice, I could see him throw his head back in laughter. He looked like a loon swallowing a fish. I was sure this story would get around the territory quicker than a boreal wildfire. Instead of waiting out the weather, and for the lake ice to break enough to get the canoes through, we packed up quickly and pushed north, as far as we could from the reserve. We paddled one canoe and towed the other. Loaded with the stove, salvaged windows, rolls of tarpaper, nails, tools and food for two months, we plodded on with only a couple of inches of freeboard between us and the deadly ice water.

Progress was interminably slow. The only open water was the channel Big M had broken with his steel boat, and a receding band along the shore. We chose the shore route because it seemed safer in case of an upset. Big M's channel was now being used by a steady convoy of Bear Islanders, each of whom would wave madly at us as they passed by in their boats, shouting something

in Ojibwa that, by exclamation, sounded a lot like "fuckin' idiots," and by this time we remained aloof and ingratiating, calculating that we didn't have much face to lose. We also didn't want anyone nosing around, looking inside our canoes and asking questions as to where we were heading.

Three long hours later we had paddled only five kilometres (three miles). Stopping abruptly at a long island flanked by ice, it was necessary for us to get out and walk to a height of land so that we could view what was ahead. It felt good to stretch our cramped legs. Once reaching a rock outcrop that faced north, with an unrestricted view for many kilometres, we paused to look out over an unyielding veld of solid ice that showed no sign of navigable breaks anywhere. No words were spoken. What made things worse, it had started to snow, covering everything in a patina of wet slush. *It may take days before the ice breaks!* I thought to myself, trying not to wear my total dismay on my sleeve. It was my girlfriend's first canoe trip and, so far, the itinerary wasn't unfolding to plan. To my surprise she didn't complain, in fact, she had already begun preparations to gather wood for a fire knowing well that we were going nowhere fast, and in the very least, we had a shaganash wood stove to help keep us warm.

That was the spring of 1973. The wilderness call was ever-present, the need to build a cabin, paramount. In fact, during a fall canoe trip, late in 1972,

Anders, Soren and myself had returned to Temagami to procure a building site for a cabin. Having been enamoured by the landscape surrounding Diamond Lake after our first trip to Temagami, and by the plenitude of building materials to be had at the old lumber camp, the location of the cabin was perfect. Using the main cabin as a base, we began a wide search for the quintessential retreat. Small Lake adjoined Diamond by two short creeks and was only three miles away to the south. After a brief foray, we knew we had found the perfect place to build the cabin. We selected a lake between Small and Diamond, closer in fact, and much prettier, easier to get building materials in and, most importantly, with good cover to obfuscate our industry. *Wapaho,* the name we applied to our little lake, was a bastardization of the actual Ojibwa word, *wapasons,* or little rabbit; it was strikingly picturesque with high hills of Jack and red pine surrounding a translucent, narrow strip of water. We would build atop a one hundred foot cliff on the east side in order to get as much afternoon sun as possible, and to have a spectacular view of the lake. A copse of thick pine would conceal the cabin from the air; we were already familiar with the bright yellow DeHavilland Beaver aircraft used by the Ontario government forestry department. No doubt, Stan Flemming, the district game warden, would be up there observing any untoward activities taking place on the Queen's property.

After clearing out a building plot, we returned to the lumber camp and began taking down the old stable. The boards were well seasoned, a full inch thick and up to a foot in width. Nails were pulled and straightened for later use, stored in an old Maxwell House coffee can. The two canoes were rafted together and the boards piled on top, barge-style, until there were only a couple of inches of freeboard left. We made three trips across the lake in the late evening, while the wind had softened and it was safe to travel. The following day, a portage was cleared and the boards shoulder-carried across and restacked on the other side. Once all the boards were portaged, we rafted the canoes again, loaded the boards, and paddled to the base of the cliff. A trail was partly cleared to the top of the cliff but kept natural near the shore in the attempt to conceal its whereabouts. The boards were heavy, long and awkward, taking two days to carry them all up to the site. They were stacked neatly and covered with plastic sheathing to keep them dry.

Anders opted to stay back at the lumber camp while Soren and I began felling red pine trees above the cabin site. Selecting the straightest trees (which was an art in itself, as the tree will undoubtedly bend when you approach with an axe), we cut a dozen pine and left them to dry on the steep slope above the building location. These would do nicely for the first few rounds, however, we failed to remove the bark from the logs; a host of boring beetles and carpenter ants would eventually make the most interesting mosaic signatures on the wood. The logs would be skidded down the hill at a later date.

Spring could not have come soon enough. I had saved up about eighty dollars over the winter to put towards cabin supplies and food for six weeks. I had made a call to Lakeland Airways in Temagami to inquire about the lake ice and was told that it would be clear in a couple of days. That was all I needed to hear. Trudy, my girl friend at the time, who truly had a spirit for adventure and an undying faith in me as a protector, agreed to go with me, much to the chagrin of both her mother and the parish minister.

Trudy wasn't a rebel until I coerced her into the wilderness. The prospect of building a cabin in the woods together was a romantic notion for two undefiled souls. She had known about my obsession about building cabins since the days of my underground hideaway when we would meet in the evenings and hang out by lantern light in the gloom tomb. All I could talk about was canoeing and how great it would be to build a secret cabin up north.

And here we were, breaking ice along the shore, canoes loaded down with a thousand pounds of gear, two platonic idealists paddling their hearts out and loving every minute of it. It took five days to reach Diamond Lake. We had left most of the building materials at the short portage into Wapaho and went on to the lumber camp where we would stay while building the cabin. And as it generally is, spring characterizes itself in a vague disguise of moods; one moment it's cold rain and searing wind with a hyperborean edge to it, and in a nanosecond it transmutes into a spectacle of cheerfully luminous weather, birdsong and optimism.

The first morning we carried most of the supplies across the short portage into Wapaho Lake and on to the base of the cliff to the secret trail that led up to the prospective building site. It took some time configuring the angle of lay for the cabin because the ground was not at all level, dropping about four feet from end to end, and guessing how visible the finished project would be from the lake. With that rationale in mind we set the front corner pillars back about twenty feet from the cliff edge; if any canoeists happened by, paddling below, they would be hard pressed to see the cabin. Although a canoe route, the water trail was not popular amongst paddlers because of the difficulty of portages beyond and south of Wapaho and Small Lake, and most canoeists rarely strayed off the beaten path—lucky for us. But throughout the project, a veil of secrecy was maintained that would be the pride of any covert secret service.

Examining the logs that were cut last fall, I discovered an audible chorus of worms and beetles chewing their respective trails under the bark. *Shit, that was quick,* I remonstrated myself for shortsightedness. Another of Nature's immutable distinctions was the ability to break down organic matter into some other usable form—trees to sawdust, home of flicker and flying squirrel, then domain of worm, ant and beetle. We quickly debarked the logs so that the sun would dry them out and the borers would vacate their premises. Still the logs, sometimes over twenty-four feet in length, were green with winter weight and had not seasoned at all. One by one, they were skidded down the rocky slope to the building site using stout ropes, slinged and pulled by hand. Even wearing gloves for protection, our hands were blistered after the first day of work.

It took an entire day just to set the sill logs in place, levelling by eye and squaring off the foundation as best we could with the few tools we had at hand, and they were: a five-foot crosscut saw, handsaw (salvaged and not overly sharp), hammer, axe and chisel. Over the next three days we managed to notch and fit into place, five rounds of logs, using up what had been cut, peeled and skidded down the backslope. The walls seemed to rise ever so slowly. The decision was made to put up only two more rounds of logs and then use salvaged boards, double-walled, to finish off the walls. We also hated the idea of cutting any more red pine trees than was absolutely necessary.

Trudy and I would work until near dark, paddle the two miles back to the Diamond Lake camp, prepare dinner by lantern light and collapse into bed, exhausted. Stud material for the walls was easy to find; the stable had been cleaned of boards the fall before by Anders, Soren and myself, and sat in a pile at Wapaho, but we had left all the 3 x 5s intact, still holding up the roof. We knocked out every other stud so as not to collapse the roof on our heads, cleaned them of nails (saving and straightening all) and carried them down to the lake. Since we had two canoes, the lumber was easily rafted across Diamond to Wapaho, and then carried across the portage, repeating the raft-and-carry procedure again at the end of the portage. Each day following, we would load up one canoe with what we could carry safely, adding to our store of materials. Within a week we had laid the floor, erected the walls, set in the windows, and hoisted three beams into place as ridge-pole and purlins. The best boards had been saved for the roof. By the end of the next week, the roof had been finished and tarpapered, and the stovepipe fitted.

We took stock of what was needed to finish the cabin, happy at what we had accomplished so far, and made plans to return later in the year to finish the job. The summer had kept us preoccupied with other things; work when we had it, but mostly canoeing the various routes throughout Temagami, sometimes stopping briefly at the Cabin Falls on the Lady Evelyn, or at Wapaho. It wasn't until late fall when we returned for two weeks to work on the cabin. We had to vacate the Diamond Lake cabin as hunters had moved in, tossing all our belongings out in the drizzle while we were over at the building site across the lake. It was quite a surprise to return to see that we had been evicted by eight gun-toting rednecks. Gathering up our gear, we paddled back across the lake to the unfinished cabin and stayed there. Worried about creating too much noise, we curbed our work and set about exploring the terrain around the cabin. We were overjoyed to discover a pure spring only one hundred yards away, at the same contour of the cabin, the water clear and earthy. This would omit the steep walk down to the lake to fill our water jugs. On the edge of the cliff, we built a fire pit and bench so that we could spend evenings by an open fire, with a clear view of the night sky.

Sad to have to leave, we packed up and headed south, unsure about how we would cope, feeling all the more distant from the mainstream. There was only a brief respite, a few odd jobs with a carpenter to earn enough money to buy supplies, and train tickets to Temagami were bought for a winter stay at Diamond Lake. Trudy would stay behind in school, and I would team up with my friend Soren. During that winter sojourn, with the ulterior motive to finish off the Wapaho cabin, we had managed to do very little. Having run out of salvaged wood to finish the double walls, and with gaping holes between the boards, the cabin was just too cold to work on. But as soon as the lakes were clear of ice, Trudy and I returned, determined to finish the job.

In March of 1845, Henry David Thoreau built his cabin on Walden Pond for less than thirty dollars. He lived on twenty-seven cents a week. Borrowing tools, he bought a dilapidated "shanty" for $4.25, salvaging boards and rough furnishings to be transported to his chosen building site on the shores of Walden:

> "I took down this dwelling the same morning, drawing the nails, and removed it to the pond-side by small cart loads, spreading the boards on the grass there to bleach and warp back again in the sun…so I went for some days cutting and heaving timber, and also studs and rafters, all with my narrow axe, not having many communicable or scholar-like thoughts singing to myself…"

Total Cost of the Wapaho Cabin, 1974

Kerosene	$2.00
Stovepipe	$4.50
Hinges & Lag Bolts	$8.00
Window Latches	$1.00
Window Putty	$0.25
Curtains	$5.00
2 Lanterns	$10.00
1 Kettle*	$4.00
Pots*	$2.00
Mixing Bowls*	$1.00
Cups, plates, glasses, cutlery*	$4.00
Tea Towels	$1.00
Thermometer	$1.25
Total:	$44.00

* Items purchased at flea markets

My cabin was larger than Thoreau's by almost one-hundred square feet; his domain was 10 x 15 feet which was quite large enough for one man, while mine was 14 x 16 feet, replete with covered front porch and a tidy strip of deck to the sun side of about four feet in width, running the length of the cabin.

Trudy and I had made several more runs to the old lumber camp on Diamond, for boards and for nails, as well as oakum chinking to stuff into floor cracks. Once the entryway and deck were finished, we set about the building of finer details, like bunk beds, table and benches, interior beam supports and kitchen counter. We salvaged an old sink from the camp and built it into the counter, running the drain pipe through the floor; the old cookstove, still sitting in the Diamond Lake cabin, was hauled over and up the cliff and united with the stove already hooked up. I rigged up a water catchment system using an old oil drum mounted outside just under the eave of the roof; water was directed to the barrel by a thin strip of wood, angled on a forty-five degree persuasion; a flexible pipe, fitted to the bottom of the drum, entered the kitchen and was tapped just over the sink. My uncle in North Bay supplied the drum and fittings.

Finally, an outhouse was erected a short distance away, the door positioned so as to allow an unblemished view of the cabin and the lake below, and a

small table to hold a wash basin was constructed. It was truly a remarkable sight. It was done—we were finished.

A bottle of wine appeared from Trudy's pack and we celebrated the completion of the cabin, sitting on the rocks at the edge of the cliff. For curiosity sake, we calculated the number of trips it took to get salvaged building materials up the cliff:

Total Board Feet:	2,000
Weight per Foot:	2 lb.
Total Weight:	4,000 lbs. or two tons

Total Distance Carrying lumber over portages:

41 kilometres (25.5 miles) (82 kilometres or 51 miles return trip)

Total Distance rafting lumber:

10 trips x 5.6 km=56 kilometres (35 miles)

In addition, thirty red pine trees were cut and skidded to the site, and six canoe loads of windows, stoves, tarpaper, and other cabin miscellany, were paddled a distance of 64 kilometres (40 miles) each trip (or a total of 386 kilometres or 240 miles).

But it had nothing to do with the heavy labour and the seemingly endless job of moving things from one place to another, ever so slowly, over the period of two years. It was a perfectly brilliant adventure with just the right additive of suspense and mystery to sugarcoat the toil.

"Let's spend Christmas and New Year's here," I almost begged Trudy. And I didn't have to pry an answer out of her. Her family and the church had ostracized us both back home, chastising me for luring Trudy away to the wilderness, and Trudy for complying to unabashedly follow. The minister had admonished me severely (I had been playing guitar for the church's religious-folk group from which I was unceremoniously thrown out for fear of inflicting my blasphemous, un-Christian misdemeanors upon the flock). The only way to atone for my sins, according to the preacher, was to propose marriage to my girlfriend; honour was a peculiarly strong association for me, but marriage? I had to ponder seriously, the implications of such a request at a time when *freedom* was my mantra. Love had little to do with it—for me, the "L" word, as it applied to a lifelong mate, simply didn't exist; Trudy and I had an unbreakable friendship where carnal pleasures were simply incidental, if at all, and we had never even discussed the possibility of partnering until forced by the Hand of God. And God, to me, as a representation of human faith, as a white-bearded male autocrat, seemed all the more preposterous. Trudy and I, clear-minded about enjoying God's green earth, innocent of any improprieties cast upon us, chose to disregard the reprove of church and family, and strike out, once again, for the wilderness.

Anxious to return to Wapaho, we kept close touch with the airways in Temagami, inquiring often about freeze-up and the possibility of flying in to Diamond Lake before Christmas. Thankfully, winter had descended upon the north earlier than usual, and Lakeland Airways had their planes on skis by the middle of December.

"The ice may be poor but we can try to get you in on the twenty-third," Bob Gareh announced, adding that I could barter the cost of the flight in exchange for some illustrated brochure commissions. It was late in the day by the time we landed on Diamond Lake, only two days before Christmas. Gareh had circled around in the Cessna over the snow pack to see if water came up through his tracks. It didn't—there was no slush but we could see small craters of open water in the middle of the lake. Lakeland Airways thought we were setting up once again in the old lumber camp cabin, like last year; they had no idea that

we were set to cross the lake to a newly built cabin on Wapaho. Gareh bid us good luck and left quickly as it would be dark within the hour.

We had to move most of our gear into the Diamond cabin and load up just what we would need for the night at Wapaho. Crossing the lake was tedious, sidestepping the open holes, feeling the thin ice give slightly under the snowshoes. In some places, the ice was only an inch thick—barely strong enough to hold our weight.

It was dark when we reached our cabin, overwrought and exhausted, but elated to have made the trip. Lanterns were lit, fires ignited in both stoves, and a makeshift dinner of soup and coffee made with melted snow water. We didn't care—all we wanted to do was sleep and not try to think of all the rest of the gear that we had to lug over the next day.

It was one of the most memorable Christmas's that I can remember. Trudy baked bread and made stuffing for the small turkey we had flown in with while I cut down a small spruce for a Christmas tree. It was decorated with small foil-wrapped chocolate balls. I played my guitar and Trudy hung our stockings on the centre support beam, mainly to deter the mice from eating any of the contents. The temperature plunged outside and the two iron stoves glowed cheery red with warmth inside. That night I slept with the bag of onions and carrots to keep them from freezing, but slept little due to the patter of little rodent feet throughout the cabin. It turned out that most of the noise came from a pair of wily flying squirrels who had found an opening in the north gable and had made themselves quite comfortable in the hospitable ambiance of the cabin. The Christmas tree had been neatly trimmed of chocolate balls, telltale shards of foil lay in little piles on the cabin floor. The first thing I did was to build a feeding shelf just outside one of the front windows; all we had to do was open the window and dump our plate scrapings on the feeder and wait for visitors to arrive.

Christmas day was a brilliant, cold wonderland, crisp of sound as the echo of the axe splitting firewood resonated off the cliffs across the lake in dull retorts. Blue jays called to each other in raucous excitement and ravens spinned in barrel rolls in the light airfoils below the cliff in front of the cabin. We had brought in rather lavish treats for the day's festivities: pickled beets, apricot preserves, sardines, mixed nuts, two cans of egg nog, and a bottle of Black Tower wine. By late afternoon, the cabin was satiated with the aroma of wood-stove-cooked turkey; a bottle of brandy was cracked as we sat and watched the humorous antics of chickadees on the feeder, passing time in a most simple and delicious slothfulness.

Dinner was an epicurean delight and we indulged ourselves until we could eat no more. Trudy had made a custard sauce for the small fruitcake that was downed with the final dregs of wine. The carcass of the bird went outside on the feeding shelf, and in no time was invaded by a troop of hungry shrews, cleaning the morsels of leftover flesh off the rib cage like piranha. We slept soundly that night as the winter cold crept in from the north; trees tightened and spoke to each other in pops and snaps and flying squirrels began using the top bunk as their landing platform before gliding down to the kitchen table where we now left a dish of nuts and scraps specifically for their indulgence.

Over the next few days, the ravens—with ever the keen eye for food—slowly picked away at the dead branches cliffside of the feeding platform until they had a clear entryway, after which they became regular visitors. And it was all this activity around our domain that reminded us that we were never alone, really, and that this was their home as much as it was ours; we all lived together on the precipice of this small northern lake in perfect harmony. Since the cabin had no name affixed to it, we chose the Ojibwa word for "little brothers"—*nitchhee keewense.* I burned the name on to a piece of board and hung the sign over the porch entryway. We liked the sound of it. Life could not have been any more quiescent.

A month later, Trudy and I walked out the seventy-two kilometres (forty-five miles) to town, climbed in the car and drove south. Finding it increasingly more difficult to cope with the prosaic life on the sheer line of the city mainstream, we made the decision to get married and move north, permanently, to where our hearts were—close to Nitchee Keewense and our "family" of familiar and applauded wilderness brethren.

Nine: Snake Creek Homestead

Freedom is just Chaos, with better lighting.
Alan Dean Foster, b. 1946

"We're going to kill you, then burn your cabin down," the man said. I could feel his hot, rancid breath in my face. We began to grapple with each other. Moments earlier, I had lunged at his friend as he flew by on a snow machine, knocking him off into the deep snow where he floundered in a drunken stupor. The others dismounted and I was surrounded.

"We don't like newcomers puttin' up No Trespassin' signs since we's bin huntin' here on this land long before yer sorry ass bought it!" exclaimed the leader of the pack. There was no sense arguing with them. They were drunk *and* doped up—a bad combination when challenged into a fight. The four men had arrived on snow machines, out of nowhere, like angry hornets, buzzing in circles around the cabin, obviously vexed about something and looking for trouble. Tempers flared. Fists were raised. And just when tensions peaked, a rifle shot split the cold air and a bullet whined over our heads.

My wife was standing on our porch cradling a Winchester 30:30 in her arms, smoke spiralling upwards from the barrel. The four men sped off in their respective machines.

Two hours later, two cops arrived and banged on our door. This was definitely not a social call. Not waiting for us to answer, they bulled their way in and began shoving me backwards into the kitchen.

"We're going to charge you with assault, and your wife with dangerous use of a firearm," the first cop announced. They were belligerent, exclaiming that because we lived so far out in the country, at the end of a dead end road, and that we didn't *socialize* with their wives (as they succinctly pointed out), we were not to be trusted. They seemed not to care whether the men had made death threats and were on private property. Behind the kitchen counter, only two steps away, was a loaded rifle; we had fully expected the "boys" to be back—not the local constabulary acting like goons! My wife began dressing down the cops but also motioned to me not to do anything.

They backed off when we threatened to take these fabricated charges against us before their superiors.

Trudy had done the right thing—*the only thing*. Firing the gun was not a practiced reaction to life-threatening situations that we had rehearsed; it was Trudy's knee-jerk attempt to diffuse a potentially dangerous calamity. We had no phone. What else could she have done? I was impressed, and thankful. I was a scrapper, but I also knew my limitations—in the north, there is no such thing as a fair fight. My wife realized this too.

After completing the Wapaho cabin, I had continued to travel the backcountry of Temagami, sometimes solo paddling, but most of the time in accompaniment of close friends or with Trudy. Realizing that we had no place to spend the winter months, which in Canada amounts to at least half the year, we began searching for land on which to build a permanent residence. After lengthy explorations on my motorcycle, and a couple of near-death incidents on black ice, I traded in the bike for a car, on top of which was strapped salvaged windows and other cabin-building accoutrement, and off we went driving across northern Ontario in search of accessible homestead land. Not having any luck at all, we ended up back in Temagami in the fall of 1976, once more making a beeline to our secret cabin on Wapaho.

With no fixed home, the appeal of homesteading as a way of life, was a natural evolution from the Spartan wanderings by canoe. Vietnam war draft dodgers were flooding into northern Canada giving rise to the popularity of communal, back-to-the-land enterprises. Most of these would invariably fail once the reality of the work required to facilitate such undertakings was realized; nonetheless, there were those that succeeded, enough at least for Trudy and me to assume that we had the right endowment to carry it out. Just the prospect of being able to *drive* to our home, maybe plant a garden, live off the land, inspired us to be diligent about the opportunity. Finding the perfect piece of homestead property was not as easy as we had anticipated—until we met Roxy Smith.

Our friend Vagn Petersen, caretaker for Camp Wabun on Lake Temagami, knowing we were searching for suitable land, introduced us to the camp cookie—Roxy Smith. Roxy was in his early seventies with thin blond hair and absolutely no facial hair. Roxy also had enormous breasts, partly concealed under a loose-fitting flannel shirt. We asked no questions. He was also executor of their family estate, four hundred acres on the Ottawa River, about twenty-four kilometres (fifteen miles) north of the Town of Mattawa. Emigrating from Ireland at the turn of the last century, avoiding the conflict between Irish nationalists and the British-backed unionists, and the ominous threat of civil war, the Smiths had landed in the United States and moved north into Canada. The Province of Ontario was offering cheap farmland in the New Liskeard area, prompting farmers to settle and grow crops for the burgeoning mining companies northeast of Temagami. Unhappy with the weather, the Smiths looked further south and found some land on the Ottawa River, just north of the historic site of Mattawa. The Temiskaming Railway was supposed to have been pushing its way north along the Ontario shore and a small village had sprung up in expectation. Snake Creek was actually a small river flowing in to the Ottawa River from the Quebec side, but the settlers commandeered the name, and for a short while, it stuck. There was a schoolhouse, a church for every major Christian denomination, and several scattered subsistence farms. When the announcement came that the rail line was to be built on the Quebec side, most of the Snake Creek residents left—but not the Smiths. With ten children in tow, they built a farmhouse out of lumber salvaged from one of the now abandoned churches and began clearing land. Farming was tough at best, but they occupied a strategic river crossing that was used by loggers and sportsmen headed for Quebec wilderness. During conscription, at the onset of the First World War, the two eldest boys were sent up the mountain at the back of the Smith property where they each built a log cabin. Roy stayed until the end of the war, while Ernest would remain reclusive until he died the year Trudy and I moved to Snake Creek in 1977.

Roxy offered us the exclusive use of a one-hundred acre parcel of land fronting the Ottawa River. Not that we could actually make use of the shoreline for there was a ninety-metre (three-hundred-foot) drop-off to the water; and it was past the maintained road, up what Roxy called "The Mountain"—where his brother Ernest still lived. I had paddled that stretch of the Ottawa back in 1970 and had committed to memory the absolute majesty of the hills framing such a magnificent historic river, dreaming whimsically about building a cabin high up in the Laurentians where the view would rival that of the gods. When Roxy proclaimed hesitantly that the price would be one hundred dollars rent per year, we accepted before he even finished his offer.

Besides Ernest, Roxy had two other brothers still living on the fraternal property: Walter occupied a closed-off portion of the old farmhouse at the end of the road while Richard, now retired from the Canadian Pacific Railway, had purchased a forty-acre parcel of land adjoining the family homestead. He lived in his cabin beside the road, about one-half mile shy of Walter. Richard was drunk most of the time, but harmless.

I had just started a job illustrating park brochures for the North Bay District office of the Ministry of Natural Resources, shortly after Trudy and I got married. We took an apartment in North Bay, close enough to commute to the new property where we would build a cabin. It was fall and we needed to commit to the project right away. Once Roxy had completed his seasonal tenure with Camp Wabun on Lake Temagami, the three of us headed for Snake Creek in our jeep. We stopped briefly to talk with Walter in the old farmhouse then edged our way up the mountain. The road was nothing more than a glorified moose trail, deeply rutted from washouts, steep and overgrown with raspberry cane, but, with some brief stops to clear fallen trees, we made it to the property.

There was one string attached to our land-lease agreement; Roxy needed a steward to oversee the entire estate. Local hunters had been roaming the property at will, even parking in front of the farmhouse, raiding Walter's garden. Walter stayed in the house afraid to come out, while the nimrods boldly partied, drank and fired rifle shots at the decrepit farm implements retired in front of the barn. There was no hydro or phone to Snake Creek so Walter lived in fear most of the time. We accepted Roxy's terms not really putting much thought in to the complexity, or danger, of policing the property. *How hard could it be?*

We now had a modest cash flow—enough to buy lumber to build a small cabin at Snake Creek, if we were frugal and creative with spending. I prided myself in being able to scrounge and barter for materials. I had basic carpentry skills, some learned while assisting a contractor in Toronto, but most acquired from practical experience. The art of wood butchery evolved from the back-to-land movement; hippies and draft dodgers building funky domiciles with nothing more than primitive hand tools. I never fancied myself as a hippy, probably because I abhorred the use of mind-altering substances, but I slid in to the genre of freedom seekers purely out of necessity to survive in poverty and my repugnance of a consumer-based mainstream.

Packing up the jeep with tools and camping gear, we drove to the property and set up camp on the bush trail, as close to a prospective building site as we could, and overlooking the steep precipice to the Ottawa River. The view was spectacular, and as Roxy had proclaimed, "You can hear the angels singing." And those angels were in full chorus. The forest was rife with both hardwoods (for fuelwood) and softwoods (for structural timber). The back slope gently eased away from the steep drop-off, mostly covered in maple and beech, with a mélange of other deciduous trees such as yellow and white birch, oak and ironwood; the beech trees wore the mark of bear claws, climbing to access the sweet beech nuts in the fall. So far, that was the only passive sign of bear. Along the bush road grew hemlock, balsam fir and spruce: several of the latter being cut and hauled to the site for sill logs. A site was excavated by hand, and levelled, and large stone foundation pads set to nest the spruce sill beams—all in the first day's work. Tired, happy, exuberant, we settled in to our small nylon tent for the night. A barred owl called somewhere on the Quebec side of the river, its voice careening through the river valley, looking for a place to rest.

Some time later, my wife shook me out of a deep sleep. "Lie still and listen," she whispered. Footsteps outside the tent—*heavy footsteps.* Someone, or something big was walking towards the tent, crisp frosty leaves crunching underfoot. Hearts pounding, we lay there motionless, not knowing what to do next. A large, ominous bulk stopped beside the tent, silhouetted by the half-light of the moon, sniffing and grunting, no more than a foot away from Trudy's side of the tent.

"Shit, it's a bear!" I said, unzipping my sleeping bag and fumbling for the flashlight. I pulled my pants on and rolled out of the tent into the cold night air. The bear was standing beside the jeep, nostrils flared, head swaying from side to side. It was staring at me. This was not my first bear encounter; when I was sixteen, during our long trip through Algonquin Park, my friends and I had run out of food and were camped on the beach near the Brent Station depot—a reprovision store. Arriving at night after being windbound for two days, we were starving, living on berries and the last of our oatmeal. We slept in the open. During the night a bear arrived, walking right over our sleeping bags, then proceeded to tear our foodpack apart. Not finding any food, it sauntered off down the lake. We weren't afraid, probably because we were much too tired to care. Not far away, a year later, three young boys were mauled to death by a black bear.

Dealing with bears is not an exact science but a somewhat unmethodical bluffing game. I ran at the bear yelling as loud as I could. It ran about forty-five metres (fifty yards), stopped, defecated, and then turned and sat down. *Now what?* I ran at it again, yelling and waving my arms over my head. It worked. The bear hightailed it down the laneway and never came back—at least that night. From then on, we slept with a couple of pots in the tent, having

to bang them on several occasions that fall while building. We couldn't wait until we had more than just a thin layer of nylon between us and a three-hundred-pound black bear.

We realized that we were in bear country. Since Earnest had died, and probably some years before while he lived in a rather crippled state, he had stopped trapping bears. Now, the old apple orchards and blackberry crops attracted them from miles around. I mentioned this to Richard who was living down the road beside the farm. He said that he had already put out a trap near the farmhouse where a young bear had become a nuisance, breaking off the branches of the apple trees.

We arrived one morning on our way up the mountain, to see a freshly skinned bear, curled up beside the road in front of the farmhouse. "Oh my god, it looks like a human!" Trudy gasped. And except for the front of the skull, it did look human. The musculature was surprisingly similar. It was discomforting. Richard took us to where it was trapped. A large, heavily toothed, leghold trap was attached to a tree with a ten-foot length of stout chain. All the brush and grass, even the bark off the tree, had been worn away, the full circumference of the length of chain. I walked over to the bear and noticed that its front leg, just above the paw, was severely mangled and torn.

"We used to just whack 'em on the skull with the back of an axe," Richard boasted, "but one mean son of a bitch knocked that axe right out of my hand and nearly took my head off. So now we just shoot 'em." It was brutal. Roxy later explained that bears had always been a problem at the farm. The family had lost several small dogs to bears. "They hate yappy dogs, the sound bothers them," he noted, relating a story of how he had looked out the window one day to see a bear carrying off their pet, tucked neatly under the foreleg, whimpering, never to see it again. I bought two guns—a 30:30 Winchester and a pump-action .22 calibre rifle. According to everyone in Mattawa we had met, we were crazy *not* to own a gun.

We managed to get a load of milled lumber up the mountain, piled in the back of a rented four-wheel-drive pick-up truck. The truck left deep, ragged ruts in the road and the fall rains soon created several washouts that made vehicular traffic next to impossible. Much of the lumber then had to be carried by hand over a kilometre up to the building site—a task reminiscent of the work we had taken on while building the Wapaho cabin.

Using a combination of logs and commercial plywood and lumber, it wasn't long before we had erected a modest 12 x 16 foot cabin. When it did snow in early November, it was a godsend; we could now haul supplies up the road by toboggan. It also meant that bears would no longer be a concern. They had managed to destroy our first camp, mostly by chewing holes in stoves and gas containers, while clawing apart anything of nylon or canvas. While camped during working weekends, we had a regular ritual of having to get up in the middle of the night to chase off a nuisance black bear. I didn't have the heart to shoot them—not after seeing the skinned-out bear that Richard had trapped.

Now that the cabin was built, we still had to secure a source of drinking water. Roxy had told us about an old natural, pure spring on the property, near his dead brother's cabin, located at the back of the hundred acres. It was about a kilometre away. Before the late fall snow, we brushed a trail back to Roy's cabin, now a mere shell with its roof caved in and a haven for groundhog and garter snake. The spring was nearby and actually quite easy to find. It hadn't been used since the 1940s, the decrepit timber liner long since rotted away and the surface thick with leaf mulch; the water still percolated and flowed vigorously from underground.

We had drinking water, albeit a nice jaunt with a five-gallon jug over the shoulder every other day, but we still had to rig up a catchment system to collect water for general purposes. Melting snow served well in the winter; when spring arrived, I would replicate the system of trapping rainwater off the roof, much like the system employed at Wapaho. A collection barrel would then gravity feed water into the sink inside the cabin.

The novelty of driving our jeep to within a mile of the cabin, and then skiing up the mountain during the winter was satisfying to us, and at first, quite acceptable beyond the initial enigma of construction in its various stages. We had started working for the Ministry of Natural Resources in Temagami. With ten days on and four days off, we retired back to Snake Creek, usually engrossed in building or improving the winter homestead. Walter had passed away while we were in Temagami, and the farmhouse now lay empty and forlorn—Walter rarely even lit a lantern at dusk. That left Richard as our only neighbour. We couldn't drive past Richard's cabin without stopping in to exchange felicitations. He made no apologies for the somewhat shabby construction of his own log cabin, claiming that he had built it from the roof down, braced by copious amounts of cheap whisky.

"D'ya want some of my homemade beans?" Richard would offer, for there was almost always a pot of beans on the back of his wood stove; and after a few days, the beans had to be chased around the black pot with a deft, quick hand. The beans, aside from being a tad dried out, were the best I have ever tasted. "Flavoured them with that bear I kilt the other day…good eh!" Richard would invariably slide out a bucket from under his bed, full of some concocted brew, skim off some of the sludge, and filter us a mug of his Irish poteen. Richard would already be well on his way to Neverland. But company was always a good excuse to have another drink, and he would entertain us with his repertoire of Irish folk songs until we had to make up some excuse to be leaving, usually to get up the mountain to light up our cabin stove before it got too late.

"Did yer notice anything different about Roxy?" Richard queried one night, itching no doubt to tell us a story. Roxy had become a trusted friend whom we would visit often, for no other reason than we found him interesting and kind. I also felt obliged to help him keep up his little house in Mattawa by doing odd jobs, reaching and lifting—things that Roxy found difficult to do on his own.

"He's a she…her name is Roxanne Smith," Richard smiled, a little full of himself. "She's also a he, b'jeesus…gotta pecker too," he added, waiting to see our response. We told him we didn't care—it made no difference to us. Roxy was a hermaphrodite. Richard showed us an early family portrait, and sure enough, there was Roxanne, posing as a little girl. "Never did them operations back then." Richard felt obliged to tell us the entire story. He poured another round of poteen and danced a jig in the middle of the floor, causing the crooked joists to heave, which eventually trembled up the walls knocking cups off the shelf. He told us that Roxanne, when reaching puberty, made the decision to dress and act like a man, working in lumber camps mostly as a cookie or dishwasher, wearing baggy clothing to hide burgeoning breasts. "It was no secret," Richard said with a trace of compassion, "everyone knew but never said nothing cuz they liked Roxy so much…always had lots of friends around." Richard fell silent and began to mope. Unlike Roxy, Richard had few close friends, and Roxy had told us to deal with Richard at arm's length. We thanked Richard for the beans and drove away, the frost having long since settled over the Laurentian landscape; the cabin would be cold and we would slide into bed for warmth, the constellations ubiquitous and enchanting.

We picked up a German Sheppard pup from a Mattawa man who claimed the bloodline belonged to a famous string of police dogs. His eight-year-old daughter also informed us that "Daddy had a freezer-full of deer meat if you want to buy some."

Mattawa was the poaching capital of Ontario, specifically for bear parts whose gall and paws commanded a high price on the black market. Roxy had not been kidding us about local hunters sneaking up the mountain in their four-by-fours, looking for game, legal or not—it didn't matter. From our cabin, we could hear any truck barrelling up the steep mountain road, a kilometre away. It wasn't long before Wolf, our dog, was ninety pounds of muscle, protective and loyal, and together we would patrol the four-hundred acres, often stopping vehicles full of trespassing hunters by blocking their path with my jeep. I would always carry the 30:30 and Wolf would snarl at the nimrods through their respective windows. Word quickly spread around town that there was a crazed wild man and his dog who didn't take kindly to hunters. And for a couple of years, living up the mountain was peaceful, without incident of any consequence, and far enough away from the main road that thievery was not an issue. We could leave the cabin without having to lock the door.

Winter came early up the mountain. By Thanksgiving there were a few inches of snow on the ground and the jeep had to be left at the road end, near the abandoned farmhouse; by mid November we were skiing. Like Wapaho, flying squirrels soon descended upon the cabin, both northern and southern variety, and squabbles over food tidbits became our regular evening entertainment. I had built a feeding shelf outside one of the cabin windows, but they

preferred to come right in and make themselves at home. Wolf would watch with bated interest as we hand fed them nuts and sunflower seeds.

By the end of the winter, nearing the warming suns of April, Trudy and I would be a little shack-whacked, anxious to get back up to Temagami and in the canoe. After the first winter, we decided to enlarge the cabin, building on a bedroom at the end of the original structure. With a large airtight stove, supported by a wood cookstove, the cabin quickly became a sweat lodge no matter how low the temperature plunged. By the third year we had had enough of the cramped living space and decided to build another cabin, just behind the first one. After improving the mountain road, enough to get the jeep up the hill loaded with lumber, we began excavating a foundation for a root cellar.

Our attempt at establishing a garden had failed miserably. The original Smith family garden plot was a kilometre away, near Roy's dilapidated cabin. After days of clearing brush and breaking the hard-packed, weed-choked ground, we had a modest plot ready to plant. Naïve as we were about the art of horticulture, and the fact that the land had long since been reclaimed by the multitude of forest dwellers, our industry was doomed to fail. Seeds were planted. We were diligent about watering and weeding. But slowly, almost with calculated audacity, our garden became subject of much activity. Bear, moose, deer, woodchucks, rabbits, raccoons, mice, voles, squirrels and an unknown number of birds, all enjoyed eating from, or trampling upon, anything that popped out of the ground, especially anything as succulent and novel as pole beans, corn or squash.

Building a fence did not work. Bears seemed to relish in the demolition of any structural perimeter, and to construct anything but a concrete bunker was an exercise in futility. We gave up trying. Nonetheless, we forged ahead with the new cabin, replete with stone root cellar in which to store *purchased* vegetables. Since our forays into town were infrequent, the cellar (excavated into the sand bank behind the original cabin) would provide storage space *and* refrigeration for perishables in the summer. A two-storey workshop, studio, and extra living space would be built above using commercial grade lumber.

We migrated back and forth between Temagami and Snake Creek, and by the fall of that year had a respectable chalet built. The new cabin-studio was heated by an oil stove in the workshop; heat would radiate up into the studio loft, while propane lights added the quintessential "northern" ambiance—irregular incandescence with a somewhat annoying hiss and asbestos mantles that continually degraded into black soot that fell irreverently on my artwork.

In retrospect, when I consider the conspicuously unhealthy living conditions under which we lived, it is with little wonder why we didn't succumb to some long-term illness. There were no widely accepted environmental concerns about the use of certain building materials, like wafer or particle-board plywood—people just put up with the chemical off-gassing; creosote and pressure-treated wood impregnated with copper-arsenate was a popular choice amongst builders because of its durability. But Trudy and I lived outdoors much of the time, which in itself was a peerless equalizer, rejuvenating the body and the spirit. Life was good. We had our Laurentian homestead, and the Wapaho cabin in Temagami to retreat to. Sanctuary seemed secure. But there was one nagging consideration—neither property was legally secure. The Snake Creek homestead was only viable while Roxy was alive; there was no authorized contract of lease for the one-hundred acres, and we had invested dearly in the two cabins built up the mountain; the Wapaho cabin was built on Crown Land and was totally illegal. There were obvious strings attached to our state of nirvana, an anxiousness that was soon to be remedied.

Ten: Paradise Under Siege

---

*The major problems in the world are the
result of the difference between the way
nature works and the way man thinks.*
Gregory Bateson, 1904-1980

The sanctity of Paradise is ephemeral, waning mercurial under the constant and irreversible mechanism of change. The avarice of corporate and consumer mainstream dictates that Paradise forfeit its treasures to the good of all. Temagami, in its uniqueness as a cultural landscape, falters under the capricious assault by industrialists and Draconian politicians. In August of 1972, the "Superstack" became operational. Inco Nickel Smelter in Sudbury, located less than one hundred air kilometres southwest of the Temagami wilderness, constructed a 1,250-foot chimney in order to disperse sulphur dioxide emissions away from the city. This vaulted Inco as the number one world source of SO_2 fallout creating more than 1% of the global airborne pollutants. No environmental assessment was carried out. Within a year, hundreds of lakes were destroyed northeast of Sudbury, including those lakes bordering the western flank of the Temagami wilderness. Fish eggs did not hatch and the trout eventually died off, water became clear as pH levels dropped, and even the great stands of white pine suffered sporadic die-back. Industry and government kept shifting blame and no political action was taken for several years. Inco threatened mass layoffs if they were forced to spend their own money on filtering emissions.

Logging companies continued to reign as unit foresters, employed by the Ontario government, which handed over large tracts of pine with careless abandon. Roads penetrated the wilderness allowing all manner of mechanized sportsmen into new territory rich in game. The Ontario tourism ministry proposed "Maple Mountain Place"—the province's answer to British Columbia's Banff Springs and Quebec's Montebello. The 78-million-dollar resort would accommodate 3,500 North American and European tourists, offering tennis, golf, swimming, horseback riding, alpine skiing and fine dining. Local politicians, including the Temagami Chamber of Commerce, applauded the grandiose scheme, claiming it would be a boost to the economy. Opportunistic politicians and short-sighted bureaucrats, glossed over the problematic factors such as isolation, rough terrain, shallow soils, bugs and climate—not to mention that it would depreciate the wilderness values enjoyed by back-country canoeists for over a century. Bear Island anishnabeg, headed by chief Gary Potts, viewed the project as a million dollar "hot dog stand" for white imperialists. It was an invasion of sacred ground to his people; *Chee-bay-jing,* or Maple Mountain, was the "place where the spirit goes after death." Claiming his band never signed the Huron Robinson Treaty of 1850 and incensed by the Maple Mountain fiasco, Potts filed a land-caution in 110 townships within the Teme-augama anishnabeg traditional lands, covering an area of 10,000 square kilometres (3,861 square miles). All development came to a grinding halt, including Maple Mountain Place, effectively creating riffs between local whites and Natives. Northerner protectionists began telling southern greens to "keep out of their business." Unfortunately, it was "business as usual" for the logging companies, intent on cutting down the last of the great pine, building their invasive webwork of roads deeper and deeper into paradise.

After having paddled Temagami extensively for six years, enjoying the sanctuary it provided, I also saw a land threatened by development. I pitched the idea of a canoe-route guidebook to the local forestry office and they liked the notion of having a comprehensive inventory of what was out there. Reg Sinclair, Lands Administrator, was also a closet environmentalist. Trudy and I were hired in the spring of 1977. After finishing a job illustrating for the North Bay District office we would start mapping out the district routes. This would take a full season to accomplish, covering an area equal in size to the Native land-caution area—10,000 square kilometres (3,861 square miles). Almost four thousand kilometres (about 2,486 miles) later, we had the information required to publish the *Temagami Canoe Routes* book, which the government printed and promoted. Sinclair realized that most of the portage trails had not been cleared for decades; Trudy and I were rehired as park rangers to facilitate a canoe-route program—maintaining and overseeing the hundreds of campsites, portages and linear routes throughout the Temagami wilderness. With the prestige and paycheque of a government job, it did not necessarily mean that things were undertaken according to the Queen's doctrine and code of ethics government employees were required to adhere to. Homesteading in

Mattawa had prepared us diligently for the job at hand—on the trail there are no written laws, just consequences.

Durst pulled the bilge plug and the aluminium boat sank, still tied to the shore. I was standing in the launch next to him, staring at the gun rack wondering what to do. The keys were in the ignition. I tossed them as far as I could into the forward hold of the boat. "They're coming!" whispered Durst forcefully, jumping off the gunwale of the sunken boat onto the shore. We could hear voices coming down the trail from the island campsite. This is crazy, I thought—I'm a park ranger—this shouldn't be happening.

Durst and I crept quickly along the shore, guided unsteadily by the light of the half moon. We found our canoe and pushed off, paddling hard for the mainland, about half a kilometre away. "Light the fire!" I yelled to Jacques who stood on the beach waiting for the signal. Seconds later, a huge bonfire erupted, engulfing a small structure that once served as a makeshift sauna. The sauna belonged to the men on the island. Flames licked high into the night sky as voices, angry voices, emanated from across the way. We managed to incapacitate only two of the three boats, and it wouldn't be long before the eight men would regroup into a lynch mob—an armed lynch mob.

My somewhat entropic lifestyle as an artist, living in a renovated chicken shack north of Toronto, grubbing a meagre living solely for the purpose of being in a canoe, came to an abrupt halt. I was now a respected civil servant, seasonal though, and married too, with a regular paycheque and a burgeoning little homestead on the Ottawa River. The salary was a bit of luck—I could canoe and get paid for doing it. Seemingly luxurious and monetarily superfluous (compared with my previous Bohemian existence), the job as park ranger would prove not only be physically demanding, but inordinately dangerous.

Trudy and I had completed the canoe-route inventory, the book was published and was doing extremely well, and we were engaged in an almost inconceivable occupation of patrolling paradise by canoe. It all seemed deliciously fantastic, romantic and, well, easy. It wasn't. Gratifying, yes, beyond my own expectations; but pathfinding came with its own eclectic fixings. For the most part, we were left alone to clear portages, clean or build campsites, and to report minor misdemeanours by recreationists—mostly fishers and hunters who were notorious for leaving behind scads of garbage and for building what the government called "UOs"—unauthorized occupations—on

Crown Land. Our job was to remove UOs. We were armed with traditional tools only—no chainsaws because the government was afraid we'd saw off our legs or some such thing. But we encountered severe blowdowns on the portages—a mélange of twisted, fallen trees that had to be cleared away by axe. It was extremely enervating work. To add to this formidable task were the vagaries of the environment: extreme weather conditions, rain wind, snow…, plus vexations of biting flies and stinging wasps.

We were to report back to the Temagami office every so often, when our two-way radio actually worked; and it only functioned if we were within thirty air miles of town and calling in from the top of a high hill on a cold morning. So, in essence, it was just added baggage to haul around. The radio, though, was an invaluable tool of authority that could be used to persuade a wilderness evildoer to bow to the Queen in dutiful servility. It mattered little that it didn't actually function. And since we travelled with nothing more officious than a crested work shirt and a radio (our request for sidearms was turned down), we had to be creative with the tools at hand. Which brings us back to the beginning of the chapter.

I had only two students with me as crew—Ken Durst and Jacques Coulombe, and our task at hand included clearing the long portages from Gamble Lake on the Lady Evelyn River, west to Smoothwater Lake. At Smoothwater we were to clean up the campsites and report on any disturbances of the back shore which happened to be a 5,000-year-old Native archaeological site. The beach campsite rivalled any south Pacific Shangri-La: white sand stretched over a kilometre beneath verdant pines; water was a translucent turquoise, and the summer sun was an elixir for tired canoeists who had toiled for days to arrive here from Lake Temagami canoe camps. This was as far as one could paddle west before rivers tipped over north or south off Ishpatina Plateau.

When we arrived at the beach we were exhausted but elated to find it deserted. I had heard that boaters were getting in to the lake by way of the Montreal River that flowed out of Smoothwater at the north end. This was bad news. Smoothwater beach was a pristine reward for hardworking paddlers; local sports nimrods were hauling bigger boats in to recreate on the beach in a supposed wilderness area. Upon our arrival I was not surprised to find an "unauthorized" shack constructed on the beach. Built of crude lumber, it was sheathed in plastic wrap, obviously to be used as a sauna. That very afternoon a flotilla of powerboats cruised to within thirty metres (one hundred feet) of the beach, consisting of eight men in two small aluminium runabouts, and a hefty cruising yacht sporting an oversized engine. The man commanding the yacht began hurling abuses at us, explicitly ordering us off the beach.

"That's our site and our sauna," levied the man, cruising back and forth but not beaching. I picked up my radio and slung it over my shoulder, took off my shoes, grabbed an axe and waded out into the water, closer to the boat so that the passengers could hear me. I explained that I was a ranger working for the government and I was sent to clean up the beach and remove the sauna.

"If we have any trouble, all I have to do is call in for backup, anytime," I lied. The radio was useless this far out. More curses from the boaters. They came to water ski off the beach. The smell of alcohol wafted to shore. And then they left and set up camp on the nearby island just before nightfall, mooring the boats on the leeside facing us.

In the dark we could hear shouting from the island. Their campfire was more like an inferno. Durst and I paddled over to scout. Beaching the canoe, we walked to within a few metres of their campsite and listened from behind a veneer of sedge and spruce. Not only were they drunk, they were hot-knifing crack, enjoying a little California sunshine in paradise. We didn't like what we heard. Several men suggested that the group "shag the mothers," and take over the beach with force. How much force, I wondered?

Returning to our own campsite, I instructed Jacques to stay behind and get ready to set the sauna on fire, while Durst and I paddle back over to see if we could disable their boats. There was just enough moonlight to navigate by. After taking out of commission the two boats, scant minutes before the men filed down to the lake, Durst and I made it to the beach while Jacques torched the shack. This smacked of Lord of the Flies, fire blazing, illuminating half-naked bodies armed with sticks and axes, disembodied voices screaming profanities of murder and revenge.

Several men had piled into the remaining boat that was still serviceable, cruising back and forth in front of us, yelling, threatening. I waded out again, axe in one hand, radio in the other, fingering the on/off switch so as to make an audible radio sound as if I had already been in touch with head office in Temagami. I warned them not to land on the beach or there would be trouble. The boaters left. The island was silent. That scared us most of all. Now what are they planning?

Thinking they would be back for sure, sneaking in to our camp perhaps with clubs or guns, we set up an "early warning" signal using a stout fishing line, strung with tin cans salvaged from the dumps, and threaded it around the perimeter of our camp. Instructing the students to sleep with their clubs and leave their door flaps open, I fell asleep sometime in the early hours before dawn. We were exhausted. When we woke the next morning, we noticed the boats had disappeared from the island. They were gone! Paddling over to the island we found a deserted, and very trashed campsite. We felt an overwhelming sense of victory. This affair would not be written into my weekly report!

In the spring of 1978, I had received a rather disturbing phone call from my friend Soren. The Wapaho cabin had been found by the government and an eviction notice was nailed to the door! Soren had paddled in with a couple of rolls of roofing asphalt when the discovery was made. I was privy to the talk amongst the staff at the forestry office and I had made the appropriate, curious inquiries about the details of the cabin discovery. There had been a lightning strike at the apex of the hill behind the cabin which, as is often the case, erupted into a flash fire at the base of a large pine. A fire-fighting crew was flown in from Temagami and dropped close to the proximity of the cabin at Wapaho Lake. On their way up the steep slope to reach the fire, the men accidentally stumbled across the secret trail to the cabin. Head office was notified, an agent was sent out by float plane, and the eviction notice posted. When Trudy and I got the opportunity to paddle to Wapaho, the eviction poster was quickly ripped off the door and burned in the cabin stove. The fire crew had left garbage strewn around the cabin and things were missing. It felt as if someone had desecrated our private space. Fire crews had a particular immunity within the government deployment; the branch enjoyed an unlimited budget for operations, and leaving a pile of trash behind at a work site was typical. Firefighters were stationed apart from the rest of the staff operations in Temagami; they operated the "warehouse," aptly dubbed the "whorehouse" by the other branches because, for the most part, all they did was play cards and breeze through stacks of *Penthouse*. Then, aside from cutting the compound grass and washing government trucks, there wasn't a lot for them to do until a fire flap. To make extra money, firefighters often "pushed" a fire instead of extinguishing it; crews were left at the site to tend flare-ups which were often instigated manually to boost overtime hours. This practice enflamed Temagami's largest wildfire in 1977, burning over 35,000 acres of prime pine.

The Wapaho cabin remained inviolate for seven years. We were all mindful not to evoke the curiosity of government aircraft by keeping stove fires burning clean and smokeless. Now, by pure circumstance, the status of the cabin changed drastically. It was this other appendage on my soul that had become infected and I didn't know how to treat the affliction. It hurt terribly. I was angry, mostly at my inability to do anything about it.

At the forestry office in Temagami I was approached by a summer, casual employee—a student assigned to the task of locating the owners of several district UOs (unauthorized occupations). His name was Ian. He asked if I knew anything about the Wapaho cabin, and who might have built it. He produced an old issue of *Field & Stream,* the very magazine I had found at a fisherman's illegal campsite about fifty miles west of the Wapaho cabin; stuffing the magazine in my pack, I had placed it on to the reading shelf of the cabin.

Priding himself to be somewhat of a sleuth, Ian had contacted the owner of the magazine using the American address affixed to it. Of course, the Yankee sportsman had no idea what cabin Ian was talking about. After hitting several blank walls, Ian began pestering me about it; he had been suspicious all along but I continued to deny any knowledge of the cabin—I was buying some time. Another year went by, at which time the government made a motion to clear out all remaining UOs in the district, and there were several, with the intention of sending in a fire crew to burn them down, regardless whether the owner removed personal items or not.

Our Temagami canoe guidebook was selling well, and the trail clearing and garbage removal program continued to hail commendations from the general public. With that accolade I confessed to my supervisor (the closet environmentalist who, no doubt, as a person of higher authority, benefited most from the approbations), hoping that I had accrued enough points to bide well with the aging district manager.

"When was the cabin built?" queried John Rumney, District Manager for Temagami. I told him that it was constructed in 1972, which was a lie, but I knew what he was getting at. The anishnabeg land caution was initiated in 1973 and no Crown land disposition was possible until the dispute with Bear Island was settled. Rumney assured me that I would receive a Land-use Permit because the cabin preceded the caution. The permit, costing less than one hundred dollars annually, would be issued the following spring. Trudy and I were ecstatic. The rumours were true—government employees did look after their own.

That same year, I had several disconcerting experiences while in the field, noticing, and reporting on a slew of logging infractions and illegally constructed bush roads. There was also inside talk that some of the unit foresters

working for the government were accepting cash bribes and gratuities from the logging companies. After our ranger work was finished for the season, Trudy and I retired to our Snake Creek homestead for the winter. Incensed about the disreputable logging practices, and the do-nothing attitude of the Temagami District office, I took it upon myself to write a letter to the minister of Natural Resources in Toronto. Bad idea. The letter ricocheted back to the district manager in Temagami. Rumney, sitting on the cusp of retirement, hated "Minister's Letters" more than anything, chiefly because he actually had to deal with it as an annoying breach of internal trust amongst the throng. Because of the letter, Rumney didn't want to hire me back; luckily, my program was successful enough to warrant reinstatement but not without consequence.

The Wapaho cabin was burned to the ground. Every board, beautifully seasoned pine logs, hand-carved furniture and fixings, paddled-in windows, inestimable days of hard labour, memorabilia, memories, all incinerated out of pure, unadulterated spite. A fine copse of healthy red pine trees, where the whisky-jacks and red squirrels would cajole and scold each other over hidden bits of food absconded from the feeding shelf, about a half-acre in dimension, also burned in the conflagration. Trudy and I had only removed one stove and a few personal items the year before. I was too angry to be disconsolate.

It was twenty years before I returned to the site, but I had seen the brown patch in the verdant pine, marking the bruise on the cliffside where the cabin stood, as I peered through the window of the float plane that passed over Diamond Lake many times since. When I did return, the outhouse was nearly intact, and small trees had grown up through the rubble; a birch sapling about ten feet in height grew through the drain hole in the blackened sink. I camped on the site for two days trying to revive some of the memories affixed to this cabin; but in retrospect, things had happened over those twenty years that in some small token way, appealed to the greater purpose that overshadowed the loss.

Once the anger subsided, Trudy and I were despondent for some time afterwards, bound by oath to get even with the Ontario government for destroying the cabin. The Temagami forestry branch had burned many remote cabins down that summer, rousing the ire of bush pilots, trappers and Natives who frequented them during bouts of foul weather. The incendiary crew was just another make-work project for the branch office with no particular purpose than to spend the allocated budget money for the year.

With the Wapaho cabin gone, I began focusing more on the Lady Evelyn cabin as a place of personal sanctuary. But I soon found out that this haven was subject to scrutiny by government bureaucrats and crayon-wielding planners. Lady Evelyn River already existed as a Waterway Park within the provincial-protected-areas plan; now, there was serious talk, finally, about expanding the park into a full-fledged wilderness park. Cabin Falls cabin existed as a privately deeded vacation property, subject to expropriation, but an expensive proposition for the government to buy out or even offer another location in exchange. As a park ranger still, and steward of Cabin Falls property, I was able to persuade the parks branch higher echelon to ignore the file, simply by proposing to the owners (the two sons of Richard Lathrop) that I be written on to the deed as a one-third owner. The Ontario government embraced the idea of establishing a "Canadian" caretaker who was willing to maintain certain standards of care necessary within a wilderness park paradigm. The Lathrop brothers, too, endorsed the concept, and for the bartered cost of a loon sketch, my lawyer prepared the necessary papers. I was now part owner of a unique retreat property.

Unbeknownst to my supervisors, I transported the Wapaho cookstove by float plane at their expense, along with my trail crew who were prepped to clear portages. Instead, we cut, peeled and floated down the rapids, several straight black spruce logs intended to be used for an addition to the cabin.

The logs were stacked and spaced, to be quarter-turned every season for a year. The addition would be built the following summer.

Tension was building between environmentalists and local forestry companies. I was working with the district Lands Planner on the groundwork plan for the new wilderness-class park—that meant that much of my time was spent in the office rather than in the field. Required to work overtime on the cartography, I was given a night key to the government office. Often, instead of working on the park maps, I would snoop through the forestry files to get a grasp of what areas were slated for clearcut logging—and there were always several sensitive areas allocated to be logged. If there was no objection from the other branches (parks or wildlife), nothing on government files to define any other use, than the timber branch could allot that forest stand to a logging company. One such area was Temagami Island, in the core of Lake Temagami and just south of the Bear Island Indian Reserve. The island contained one of the province's most remarkable stands of old-growth red and white pine trees—some over four-hundred years old; if the logging companies had their way, the island would be devastated.

Between my closet-green supervisor, Reg Sinclair, and myself, we hatched a plan to initiate a series of hiking trails in all sensitive areas, including Temagami Island, Maple Mountain and the large island encapsulated by the north and south channel of the Lady Evelyn River. The Lady Evelyn proposed cut was much too close to Cabin Falls. The proposals were quickly filed and distributed amongst other branches of the government office. Not without a show of disapproval, the timber foresters were disgruntled but subject to abide by internal policy—timbering plans were scrapped and my crew was sent in to construct Ontario's first old-growth forest hiking trail.

Blocking logging plans became a priority, and between Sinclair and myself, we successfully deflected logging companies away from prime sites, simply by building or proposing to build hiking trails. All of these put undo pressure on government unit foresters who were paid to supply logging companies with their annual required wood fibre. Now they had to look elsewhere. And as tensions mounted between "greens" and "browns," a clear distinction was cast amongst sparring partners. Within the government office, the Timber Branch rarely communicated with Parks Branch—a classic example of a breach in the law of cosmic duality—the left hand didn't know what the right hand was doing at any given time. Northerners hated southern tree-huggers and locals hated the Indians for locking up the district in a land dispute.

After the season came to a close and Trudy and I retired to Snake Creek, the need to visit Cabin Falls in the winter was gnawing at my soul, enough to book a ski-plane flight in late January bound for Dry Lake, about ten kilometres (six miles) upstream of the cabin. Spontaneous solo excursions were nothing out of the ordinary for me, but this was the first winter venture deep into the new park territory since the 1940s, and my premier visit to the cabin on the falls outside of the paddling season.

Leaving my skis on Diamond, several kilometres to the south of the cabin, where I would pick them up on my way through, the pilot dropped me off on Dry Lake with my snowshoes and a backpack, just off the river, knowing that the ice would be secure. It was late in the day, but with the cabin only a few kilometres downriver and knowing that the cabin and wood stove awaited, I pushed hard through the deep, loose snow, working up a sweat as the light waned, passing a fresh wolf kill along the way. To my horror, someone had left the north-facing window open and snow had drifted in, filling the entire cabin, burying the stove completely. Working quickly, warding off a chill, I evacuated the snow away from the stove and lit a fire, but the heat did little to warm the cabin until all the snow was shovelled out and the front door finally closed. I was frozen to the bone, cursing the soul who had left the window wide to the elements. It took another full day to thaw the inside of the cabin enough to elevate the environment to any tolerable comfort zone. Once the log walls had been warmed, the cabin lanterns gave off a welcoming ambience and I felt at home. Until then I had only used the cabin sporadically, feeling somewhat disconnected from it because it did not belong to me and I didn't take part in its construction. It was someone else's place, replete with ghosts yet to be exorcised. And it sorely needed remedial carpentry work and rechinking. Now it was mine—at least in part, and the Americans rarely came up, and the government couldn't touch me. It was the first time I had ever owned a piece of land, albeit—a choice taste of paradise. The lantern light flickered, caught by a rogue draught that invaded a dozen cracks in the walls, under the loosely hinged door, and through uncaulked windowsills. Hot tea boiled on the stove and the smell of damp clothing hung to dry, filled the cabin with my own idiosyncratic personality. I was starting to feel at home.

Eleven: Transcendence

Homesteading and the Zen of free-living out of a canoe came with a particular disposition of responsibilities, and a strict adherence to faith. And faith has as many shades as weathered barn board in twilight. Neither a religious, or openly spiritual person in my youth, I depended almost wholly on the skin of my teeth and a healthy dose of gut feeling to make things work. I had lost faith in organized religion because of the hypocrisy of its flock and the audacity of its tenets in the face of Nature. Aboriginal, or shamanic religion interested me but I remained agnostic, yet searching for some absolute truths to consolidate my own faith. I had faith in myself, with conditions of course, with room—plenty of room—for error. Faith in humankind, or the "system" continued to wane and I plodded on with a rather narrow vision of existence with a heavy slant towards survivalism. My focus concentrated entirely on daily needs and chores, of which there were many. It was a labour-intense lifestyle requiring unconditional dedication—the price of freedom. Religion was for those needing a quick fix to salvation from earthly drudgery. Heaven was paradise for the do-gooders; to me, paradise was untrammelled wilderness that was quickly being destroyed by the righteous. Yet, a deeper meaning to my life eluded me. Beyond the pragmatic, physical life of homesteading, there was a great spiritual presence somewhere just beyond reach. But in 1980, two hallmark events would change my life forever. It would profoundly alter the way I viewed life, and death, and my own mortality. Nothing would ever be the same.

It was difficult to determine the hour of night the ghost entered the bedroom of the old farmhouse. It was a twilight wakening; conscious and lucid I had no sensation in my body at all. I could move my head slightly to the right,

towards the apparition taking shape at the side of the bed. I could blink but breathing was laboured. There was a great weight on my chest and I felt as though I was being pushed into the bed by some malevolent presence. I panicked. There was an old woman leaning over me, looking at me with steely blue eyes. I was detached from my physical body; the normal signals that initiate movement were momentarily severed and I watched in utter horror as this wraithlike vapour hovered beside me. Slowly regaining the feeling in my arms, I reached up to touch the ghost, or to fend it off—I'm not really sure which, except that when I did move, Trudy woke up. "What the hell is that!" she exclaimed. And that expletive was the most horrifying because it authenticated the spirit essence at the bedside as something we were both experiencing. *It wasn't my personal hallucination.*

Sleep paralysis, or old-hag syndrome as it is more commonly known, is one of the most frightening paranormal phenomena. A demon, ghost or SMP (sensed malevolent presence) sits upon the victim's chest causing paralysis, restricting breathing, accompanied by the sensation of falling. In Thailand, people refer to being *Phi um* (ghost covered), and *Phi kau* (ghost possessed); in Japan, *kanashibara* (to tie with an iron rope); and in the far north, *komiarik* (a soul takes possession of the paralyzed victim). It leaves a person open to hallucinations, paranormal experiences and even the ability to soul travel.

I knew nothing about sleep paralysis and I didn't necessarily believe in ghosts—until then. Roxy Smith had put the old farmhouse at Snake Creek up for sale for forty thousand dollars, and Trudy's mother was interested in purchasing it. The estate would keep three-hundred acres and sell the farm and the one-hundred acres on the Ottawa River. Roxy had given us the key to check out the condition of the house; out of curiosity, we decided to spend the night there despite the fact that none of the family heirlooms had been removed. I don't know what compelled us to do this.

Roxy's brother Walter had cordoned off the upstairs and had lived on the main floor for several years because it was easier to heat in the winter. It was a still evening, moonless and cool. The farmhouse exuded an ominous but not unfriendly aura; it was like entering a mausoleum. We lit one of the oil lanterns in the kitchen and sat for a while pondering which of the five bedrooms we were going to sleep in. Taking down the shroud that closed off the upper floor, we ventured upstairs, armed with a couple of flashlights. It smelled musty, as if the years of disuse had layered everything in a patina of tired dust and stale memories. The bedrooms were tiny, reminiscent of the era when the only heat filtered up through grates in the floor. Trudy and I took what looked to be the master bedroom at the top of the stairs. The ceiling was less than seven feet high and the room large enough to barely contain a small, steel-frame bed, a nightstand and a cedar chest. It felt as if we were acting out the quintessential horror flick, faces outlined in deep sardonic shadows, cast from the wavering incandescence of the oil lamp, the floor boards creaky in a classic haunted mansion. We dusted off the mattress and made up the bed with our own blankets, climbed in and laughed ourselves to sleep.

After we had both seen the she-ghost, we sat up for some time, silent, scared and unable to sleep. The experience had a far-reaching effect on us both, instantly verifying the existence of an afterlife—not a mundane, everyday occurrence. The ghost had vaporized once I had touched it and Trudy had spoken out—the spell was broken; the thin veil of existence between the corporeal world and the spirit world had been bricked over again.

We didn't tell Trudy's mother that she was buying an authentic haunted house. We questioned Roxy about the bedroom but never mentioned the ghost experience. We were, in fact, sleeping in the master bedroom; the last time it had been used was back in the 1940s during his father's wake and Roxy's mother (who did have blue eyes) sat vigilantly at her husband's bedside in mourning. Now that Trudy and I realized the ghost was not evil, we felt almost honoured to have had the experience. Years later, after her mother had moved in, stories began surfacing about the "lady" of the house who appeared regularly, usually at the foot of the stairs, or in the master bedroom.

After making a few dollars on the sale of the family farm, Richard Smith decided to sell his forty acres down the road. He told us that he was tired of people stealing his firewood that he had cut and piled by the roadside. He had packed 12-gauge shotgun shells into holes bored in some of the wood so that when the culprit's stove exploded, he would know who was lifting his winter wood. Word got around fast in the town of Mattawa.

It was a choice piece of property, if you discounted Richard's cabin, with a two-thousand foot frontage on the Ottawa River, a riverside hunt camp (which at the time of purchase was just a plywood shell), and a driveway. *A driveway!* What a novelty to be able to drive right to our back door. Before Richard could go to town to list the property with the real estate broker, I went to the bank and took out five, one-hundred-dollar bills, stopped at Richard's on the way home, and laid the money out on the table. It had been some time since Richard had seen that much money. Sober, Richard signed a deal with me that evening; we would pay him full price for his property—twelve thousand dollars. Richard slid the poteen barrel out from under his bed and we consummated the sale of his property.

Moving down the mountain to the shore of the river was a blessing, just in the relief of not having to hand-haul everything some distance uphill. We left the cabins to be salvaged for wood by Trudy's stepfather who had moved into the haunted farmhouse. Using the hunt shack as a base structure, we built around and over it, pounding in a sand-point well, and wiring up a 12-volt power system that could be charged with a gas generator. Richard's cabin was used for storage; included in the mélange of antiques and collectibles scrounged from local auctions, were two oak barrels. The first winter we stayed at our new location was a particularly lean one, having spent our savings on building materials. During a three-day blizzard, while two friends from Temagami were bound by weather to stay over, with few groceries and no refreshments, we re-membered the two oak barrels sitting in Richard's cabin. Knowing that whisky was often stored in oak barrels, two of us walked through the winter blast over the half kilometre to see if there was any libation that could be salvaged. We were desperate. Popping the wooden bungs, we poured out the contents of the barrels into a large pan covered with a pair of Trudy's pantyhose. Bits of charcoal glistened on the surface of the stocking as good Canadian whisky filled the half-gallon pot. Jubilant, we marched back to the cabin with our prize, much to the delight of everyone, and we drank merrily the remainder of the night while snow piled high over the Laurentian landscape.

Life was good. Trudy and I continued to work as park rangers in Temagami through the summer months, and homestead on the Ottawa River through the fall and winter. We managed to revive Richard's garden, and even salvage a modicum of produce left behind by scrounging animals. Twice a day, the Temiskaming train would pass on the far side of the river, over a kilometre away—the very rail line that was supposed to have been built through Snake Creek almost a century ago but wasn't, chugging past, sounding its whistle in friendly gesture.

Life was anything but prosaic. We still had the occasional gun battle with local nimrods who would park on the back road and set up shooting targets in a nearby gravel pit. Stray bullets still found their way through the trees over the cabin, to which we would respond by letting loose a volley of 30:30 rounds in the general direction of the shooters. Truck doors would slam and they'd be off spinning gravel down the road, hightailing it back to Mattawa. Our German Sheppard dog physically escorted a trespassing hunter off our property by leading him to the property line, jaw clamped down on his gun arm until given the signal to "let go." We were living in a poacher's Shangri-La with a high population of both deer and bear residing along the river. One day our dog never came home. We did come across baited leg-hold traps just off our property, suspecting that hunters had killed or poisoned him.

But these were isolated incidents, and we could leave our cabin unlocked for days and not worry about thievery. Winters were long, the snow deep and the night firmament thick with stars. As they did at the Wapaho cabin, flying squirrels became regular visitors—both northern and southern varieties, and we could stand out on our front porch and let them land on our shoulders and take sunflower seeds from our hands. With the coming of March, La Cave hydro dam, located about thirteen kilometres (eight miles) downriver, would drop the water level of the river by twenty vertical feet in order to take on the winter meltwater. This left great slabs of thick ice on the shore slopes, but the river itself would be clear of ice. And with the warming sun, melting snow, and open water, the urge to get the canoe out on the river was always a spring ritual.

Nearly drowning in that great river was a rude awakening for me. I had always fancied myself inviolable, capable of pitting my indomitable will against any challenge. But being ignorant of the omnipotent power of Nature, as I was then, could only provoke disaster. As a Christian-raised youth, I was taught that "man should rise above nature, and to usurp her bounty." Didn't Katherine Hepburn remonstrate Humphrey Bogart in the *African Queen,* telling him that "they were put on this earth to rise above nature?" All the immutable inferences were there, stamped in memory with indelible ink.

There was only one life jacket in the canoe so I gave it to my twelve-year-old brother-in-law David to put on. Leaving from our cabin, we crossed the black, frigid water of the Ottawa River and made our way up the back eddies on Snake River, on the Quebec side. It was a gloriously warm March day and snow had been melting off the south-facing slopes, exposing granite ledges and winter-dry blueberry sedge. Thick, broken shore ice glistened in the sunlight, heaving and crackling as it melted. Snake River was a mad torrent, spilling over a thirty-metre (one-hundred-foot) waterfall, then rushing pell-mell out to the Ottawa River in wild, breaking haystacks and hydraulics.

I barked at David who was perched in the bow seat, to kneel down and brace for an eddy turn into the fast current; his legs got stuck and the front of the canoe ambled precariously across the sheer line of cross-currents. The canoe flipped and we were sucked into the main flow of water.

The water temperature was near freezing; the shock of it hit me like a sledgehammer, so hard as to dispossess all the air in my lungs in one belch. I was under the canoe for several moments without any buoyancy but managed to pull myself out by gripping on to the gunwale of the canoe. David was floating along on the same side of the boat, looking at me for directions. *I couldn't talk.* The shock of the cold water on my torso expunged all the

air in my lungs, like a deflated balloon; trying to breath was painful, like sucking air through a blocked straw. I managed to wheeze out instructions to "Let go of the canoe and swim to shore," contrary to the Canadian Red Cross water safety rule commanding you to "stay with your overturned boat until rescued." It was March—nobody was on the river, and nobody lived anywhere close. My own cabin was over a kilometre downstream, on the Ontario side and the Ottawa River was more than a kilometre wide here. Snake River, or Snake Creek as it was known, was the point at which the Temiskaming rail line went inland, paralleled by an old bush road that led to a couple of fishing camps, used only during the summer months. Other than that, the Quebec side of the river remained wild and undeveloped. Knowing that rescue was not an option, and that we could survive only a few minutes in that cold water, I made the decision to swim to shore, just as the last point of land appeared, the distance away increasing each second as the current pushed us out into the Ottawa. As I slipped off the canoe I felt myself sinking—*I couldn't feel my legs!* I began to panic. *I was going to drown…a fool's death…and Trudy was going to look out the window and see our overturned canoe float past the cabin!*

It is true, that the moment before impending death, your life *does* flash into your consciousness. And I realize that you either succumb to the distress by doing nothing, or you find the moral fibre to survive anyway you can. Anger snapped me out of the momentary fixation on my own death.

David was dog-paddling slowly against the strong current, trying to edge over to the calm water near the shore. I was beside him, trying to prompt him to keep going. "Swim…swim hard!" I wheezed. "Head for the break in the ice!" Giant slabs of river ice hung in slanted wafers along the shore, impeding access to the land, except for one split that exposed a dry beach. I was losing the feeling in my arms which were working feverishly to keep myself afloat, and it wasn't until I felt the river bottom press up against my chest that I realized that I had beached myself like a whale. I reached out with the last of my strength and helped pull David ashore. The sand felt warm, and we lay there for several minutes until the feeling returned to our limbs. We were both in shock.

We still had to rescue the canoe before it floated past our cabin. We were stranded on the Quebec side of the river—it would be two months before anyone came by, and Trudy only knew that we had gone out for a short paddle. The train wasn't due by for several hours, but there was the old road that led past a trapper's cabin, and I remembered seeing an old canoe sitting on top of a shed. The cabin was well over a kilometre inland. We jogged to stay warm, retrieved the canoe—a beat-up, aluminum *Sportspal*, and portaged it back to the Ottawa River. My own canoe was about a kilometre out from shore, in the middle of the Ottawa, drifting downstream, and I pictured the two of us still clinging to the gunnels, dead to the world. At least we had the sense to swim to shore.

We towed my canoe back to the Quebec side and returned the Sportspal to its owner. The reality of the events finally sunk in and I began to shake. I could barely get back in my canoe. Suddenly, the Ottawa River looked tremendously huge and foreboding, and my canoe inappropriately small. In front of David, I remained stoic, trying to laugh the whole experience away. The trip back to the cabin was silent. And silent I remained, David too, as shock turned to embarrassment. That secret was consolidated for several years.

The acceptance of your own resident weaknesses, I realized—the hard way—brought about a greater sense of values. The worth of your own self could be measured only as a small part of the sum of all the other facets of your life and the world that encapsulates it. I was mortal. The capricious and unforgiving nature of Nature painted a clear picture in wide brush strokes. If I was going to survive within the framework of my chosen lifestyle, I would have to humble myself to the greater power. Death, as the spectre lingering beside my bed in the old farmhouse, and near death, as a flash of memories preceding the ultimate failure, sparked a more cognizant realization that there was much more to learn about myself, about Nature and, ultimately, about life itself.

Twelve: Civil Disobedience

And at that very moment, we heard a loud whack!
From outside in the field came a sickening smack
of an axe on a tree, then we heard the tree fall.
The very last Truffula Tree of them all!
Dr. Seuss—*The Lorax*, 1971

The helicopter banked forty-five degrees left and dropped altitude below the treeline nearly atomizing the tops of the giant pine that crested the high ridge. Chee-skon abikong Lake, or "place of the huge rock lake," loomed below, framed in along the eastern shore by a sixty-metre (almost two-hundred-foot) cliff. The conjuring stone stood out in bas-relief, shadowed against the white granite. It was impressive to see from this perspective—it was impressive to see at any angle.

Two government men sat across from me. The forester was talking vigorously into his headset microphone, pointing his finger out the window and querying me for a response. I tapped my headset. It buzzed then crackled to life. The manicured voice of the forester droned feverishly over the air. "These pine are over-mature, it's a decadent forest. It's a waste if we don't get in to harvest them…we can eliminate the visual impact by cutting through the valleys and reducing the harvest along the ridges." The forester sat back in his seat, loosened his safety belt, and waited for my response. I tapped my headset again and shook my head. The forester nodded in recognition of my microphone malfunction and continued talking to the other passengers. *Why argue against total ignorance I thought. I was playing their game by their rules—a lesson in environmental futility.*

By this time, the company man sitting beside me, a local mill-field advisor who remained silent until now, spoke as if on cue from the forester. "I just don't understand you canoeists, you never get off the water anyway. If we cut the ridges, it'll be green again in a couple of years. What's the big deal?" I wanted to pounce on this assertion, even though common sense, spiritual reverence and moral conviction were deficits amongst the coterie of officials.

"Green isn't good enough," I responded out of suppressed courtesy. "Tourists from around the world come here to see the ancient pine and a beautiful skyline. You're replacing it with something inferior—a monoculture—not to mention creating access and damaging the environmental integrity of a unique ecosystem. It's not the same—canoeists won't come back, neither will the original forest."

The logger looked to the government forester for help.

"I believe what Mr. (X) is getting at is, through proper mitigations, selective harvesting, maybe the application of specialized chevron or checkerboard cuts, we can minimize the impact and satisfy both parties here." The logger nodded in compliance with the forester's rhetorical monologue. "Skyline reserves are impractical," added the forester, now on a roll, "some of the vistas from the canoeists' perspective are incredibly penetrating, several miles in fact. We can't reduce the wood fibre inventory that extensively." I couldn't help rolling my eyes; it was perfectly acceptable, though, to reduce the inventory of pristine canoe routes, remaining vestiges of old-growth forest and internationally acclaimed cultural treasures.

The other government man, sitting diagonally to me, was a regional planner. His complacent, sure-of-himself demeanor before take-off was now interfaced with a "heads-between-the-knees," utterly horrified, green complexion. The helicopter banked right, tight enough so that the lake appeared below us through the side window, shifting everyone earthward in their seats. The planner was now searching my eyes for pity. I handed him the barf bag with a wry smile. I was starting to enjoy the flight.

The pilot, Len McTaggart, was old-school-smart, as far as bush pilots go. In his late fifties and just about as fed up with government bureaucracy as I was, McTaggart played his part well. He used to fly my crew in to remote sections of the Temagami wilderness when he was flying turbo-Beavers for the Ministry of Natural Resources. We chatted briefly before the flight about the "old-days" and about all the bullshit coming down, lamenting about the loss of wilderness and how the lakes had been fished out and game was getting scarce because there were too many new logging roads being built. Len could pick out the "faint-of-flight" personalities and I sensed that he didn't like the planner either.

I dozed off, mesmerized by the seemingly endless vista of pine-studded hills and reminisced about my first canoe trip to this mysterious Land of Shadows—"Grey Owl Country"—thinking about the thin slices of bread dipped in corn syrup at McConnaghy's house, going over the old 1923 tourist map of Temagami. The leading caption ballyhooed a wild place, full of adventure, mystery—*and a proclamation of incorruptible sanctity...* :

> A magnificent area of pine-lands constitutes the Temagami Forest Reserve. Stretching one hundred miles from the north to south and ninety miles from east to west, it comprises a virgin territory of nearly four million acres. No settler or lumberman has ever been nor will be allowed to despoil it of its wooded wealth. Each rugged promontory and towering hill, the watered valleys and rocky islands remain as they were centuries ago, clothed with the forest primeval.

What the hell happened? How had things within my world—*my sanctuary*—become so complicated? How had I gone from park ranger to tourist operator—whip-dog, front man for the environmental movement? And my beloved Temagami, succumbing to wanton greed and avarice, being hacked apart by callous industrialists one tree at a time.

The ranger program had been almost entirely decommissioned by 1983. The Ontario government was more interested in opening up as much wilderness to sportsmen as possible, and that meant more logging roads, which, of course, "carte blanched" intense clear-cut logging practices. The province was trying to boost the sale of game licences and placate to the whims of local and provincial hunting and fishing organizations. At the same time, it was selling off huge tracts of Ontario's provincial tree—the white pine—a tree that commanded a high price at the mill but as of yet to be replicated through reforestation or any other silvicultural practice.

A new District Manager had swept through the forestry office, clearing some of the dead weight and putting Reg Sinclair, my closet-green boss, as far from the public domain as possible. I had a new boss—the Fish and Wildlife Supervisor—who, ten years ago, had berated Soren and I when we arrived in Temagami to spend the winter on Diamond Lake. The Ranger program was slowly being phased out and I was forced to carry out irrational work projects until it nearly came to blows involving the District Manager, Flemming and me. In 1984, I quit the service, looking forward to occupying myself with writing and art ventures. But that was not to be; Bob Gareh, owner of Lakeland Airways, coerced Trudy into convincing me to go into the outfitting business as partners. It was no small undertaking; and for me, the commitment challenged the freedom I had brandished as a ranger and homesteader. But there were also huge advantages to being a tourist operator too—like tormenting the local forestry department to whom I still vowed an oath of revenge. And there was the new park—Lady Evelyn Smoothwater Wilderness Park—a joke really, because it was far too small, and the arbitrary boundary lines drawn, clearly demarcated zones of timber extraction. The fight to preserve a "buffer" around the park would be fought in boardrooms and in the field. And my expertise lay in the field.

A consortium of paddlers and activists created the Temagami Wilderness Society, and we soon discovered that Temagami had the last remnant old growth pine stands in North America. Saving the pine tree became the consolidated mantra of a handful of activists, who would stick their necks out to do whatever was necessary to curb indiscriminant clear-cut logging in Temagami. Within two years my company had grown to be the most successful canoe-outfitting company in northeast Ontario. That made me a somebody in the eyes of the provincial officialdom, and our environmental group needed someone to slap their name on press releases as a northern tourist operator whose business was threatened by local logging. I was put on a government committee, along with the reeve of Temagami, the president of the Ontario Anglers and Hunters Association (who had fishing infractions within the new park), various business representatives and a couple of token environmentalists. Typically, these ad hoc committees were seriously skewed towards industrial interests, but the government was obliged to at least attempt to eke out a common ground arrangement between warring factions. That was like putting a pack of starving wolves in a pen with plump, acquiescent rabbits and asking everyone to get along. And so, as part of my civic duty and committee appendage, I boarded the helicopter for a look-see over the sacred, ancient forest about to be annihilated.

Len McTaggart landed the Huey 500 on the beach at Wakimika Lake and shut off the engine. The passengers spilled out of the helicopter and gasped for air that wasn't ripe with puke and jet fuel, stumbled for footing in the deep sand, disoriented and a bit shell-shocked from the noise, and gathered around the government forester to hear his next monologue. There was talk of a road, and of cutting swaths through the valleys, and mitigations and signage, and everything will be done according to ecological propriety. Len sat on a firepit log, smoking a cigarette, looking out across the wave-streaked lake, and filling in his time before retirement in a sort of relaxed euphoria.

HAP WILSON 2001

I stood beside him, away from the coterie of officials, and we both laughed saying much without saying anything at all. In three years time there would be fifty tents pitched on the beach and over a hundred and twenty-five activists prepped for civil disobedience, including the soon-to-be premier of Ontario, Bob Rae, and a number of international press agents. The International Union for the Conservation of Nature would list the Lady Evelyn wilderness as an endangered space, vaulting the Temagami logging issue into orbit as a global entity. Local foresters now had to be accountable for their sins. Sportsmen no longer ruled the back roads, although new ATV (all terrain vehicle) roads were being punched into new territory each season, illegally. Provincial officials turned a blind eye and poachers, once again, got the upper hand chiefly because they were smarter than conservation officers on patrol.

Attempting to operate a tourist business dependent on the preservation of wilderness was an adventure in pure dogmatism. My wife and I were bound to fail, one way or the other, either through some technical miscalculation in business management, or outside tampering. The act of having to lease land, owned by the local iron ore mine, to run our business developed into a subversive plot headed by town officials to shut us down. After five years of building up a company in which the town directly benefited economically, the mine terminated our lease without any explanation. The mine manager later explained that he didn't want an environmental activist leasing land from him. After the local lumber mill was closed (not because of the green movement, but through financial mismanagement), the mine manager feared that activists would go after the mine. And certainly with good reason, as it turned out a few years later when the mine did close down that several major environmental infractions had been perpetrated.

Trudy and I moved our business out of town to a small lot we had purchased for our house. We had had to sell the Snake Creek cabin because of break-ins and the necessity of spending most of our time in Temagami, glued to running the business and fighting the good fight. We built a four-season lodge, brought in a float plane from Sudbury Aviation, and became totally self-sufficient with absolutely no ties to the village. The environmental movement escalated—so did the number of thefts, abusive phone calls and death threats. Even the local constabulary kept up their constant harassment of our customers by questioning them and extracting unwarranted information. During the blockades when our new lodge became command central for the Temagami Wilderness Society, and we had connected a two-way radio system with the blockade camp on Wakimika Lake, our phone lines were tapped. Undercover police attempted to infiltrate the movement, creating a paranoia that pervaded the operation of the blockade camp and our own business. The late Gary Gallon, environmental and social activist who was then advisor to the Minister of the Environment, told me that the Ontario government was screwing around with my funding needed to finish my lodge. Monies guaranteed never materialized, forcing us into expensive bridge financing. Trudy and I could not keep up the pace.

In 1990, our business and marriage failed, not because we didn't work persistently at both, we simply burned out, lacking the energy to maintain the high-level input to make things work. Bad financial advice culminated in bankruptcy, my personal life was in a tattered ruin; I was despised by the locals for being a tree-hugging, dirt-worshipper, and the weekend warriors from the south vanished into oblivion. The Wapaho cabin was gone; my homestead was gone; my business and lodge had been swallowed whole by the chartered banks—*I had nothing left.*

I did have time. Unencumbered by obligation or commitment, I had recommissioned my absolute freedom. Having lost everything, I still owned two of the most important things in my life—my freedom and, by sheer luck, the cabin on Lady Evelyn River. I had woven my future according to my original existentialist beliefs, that without freedom, I had nothing. And freedom is such a multifarious condition that modifies all of our emotions—love, hate, envy, and pride, all inextricably entwined within the fabric of liberality. I had realized that I was married to pride, most of all, and my wife was deprived of true love because I loved the "cause" more than her; and I was infatuated with wilderness in its raw, unblemished purity of purpose because it assuaged my own need for "connection"—something devoid in my life as a child. What was sanctuary after all—a physical place—a memory?

I paddled in to Cabin Falls alone. I needed to be alone. It had been a bad winter and I needed to repair my soul. It was a cool, May afternoon when I arrived, late in the afternoon. Winter wrens warbled their trill melodies of love as I carried my pack to the cabin. The din of rushing meltwater seethed with welcoming pomp and the cabin stood, resolute and proud. Nothing had changed. I lit the wood stove and moved my chair so that I could feel the heat on my back; the warmth felt like a friendly hug, and I fell into slumber easily and long. It was dark when I awoke, slumped in the chair, the fire out, but the cabin was not cold and the river still ran past my window.

Thirteen: Conflagration

A little fire is quickly trodden out;
Which being suffer'd, rivers cannot quench.
Shakespeare, *1564-1616*

I n the north there is a clandestine network amongst some of the back-woods folk that rivals the best intelligence resources of the CIA. Northern poachers know exactly the routine movements of the paltry few game wardens spread across the district, and move easily, with stealth, through the opaqueness of night. After five o'clock, when the officers have filed their reports and have gone home, local troglodytes are out jacklighting for deer, or netting walleye with impunity. Freezers are always full in the country and the Chinese well supplied with animal parts, cum aphrodisiacs. Housebound wives radio their four-wheeling husbands on CB transmitters whenever the game wardens drive through their respective town in their green, government pick-up trucks. It's a primitive system but it works with efficient perfection. The Quebec government hired poachers to catch poachers—not far removed from the days of bounty hunters—killers hired to catch killers.

My uncle's second wife's father was the mayor of the northern village of Elk Lake back in the 1950s. Elk Lake is a struggling logging town located at the northern periphery of the Temagami wilderness. For a while, anyone travelling through with a canoe on the vehicle roof would not be served gas at the local station. Townsfolk hated environmentalists and canoeists, blaming them for the creation of the wilderness park, which effectively shut down that region for logging and hunting. The current mayor is a descendant of my aunt's family, and that juxtaposition makes us some sort of distant cousin, removed or otherwise. The hippy-hating mayor did not easily digest this bit of trivia, but I thought he should know that I was part of the "family." Disgruntled loggers and hunters threatened to burn down the park (whose boundary lay slightly more than 48 kilometres [30 miles] to the south of the town), and were incensed that I should own the only patent deed in the reserve; railing to the effect that I was unfairly granted my own personal sanctuary of over

2,590 square kilometres (1000 square miles). In their minds, I enjoyed the gratuity of government favouritism. To me, it was luck of the draw, and the government just happened to have built a park around my cabin, which, of course, was built fifty years earlier.

Once a debutant moves into a northern village, he (or she) is quickly sized up and fitted into one or the other camp—green or brown—and put on intercommunion probation. It doesn't take much to establish which of the two camps you'll find yourself in—a bumper-sticker, attire habits, slogan on a T-shirt, or a letter to the editor of the local newspaper could get you ostracized from the general social mélange. Regardless of how plausible or non-partisan your political views may appear, in a northern logging town there is no neutral ground. Apathy hangs like a pall within the social aura of a sunset-industry town because they are almost always on the brink of collapse. Change is as welcome as a pack of wolves at the back door—an apparent cause of the five hundred or so ghost towns across northern Canada. Industrialists move in and immediately infiltrate the social stratum of a small town, make promises of a good life for the minions, quickly establish a "big brother" fiefdom, and speak nothing of exhaustion of resources, environmental impropriety, or—change. When the mine, or the logging mill, shuts down, usually on its own volition for economic reasons and world market prices, the townsfolk blame whoever might have recently aroused their ire, and environmentalists in the north are easy prey for attack.

It was no secret that I owned a piece of paradise in the wilderness park. This sat like an undissolved lump of memory in the craw of local, displaced loggers and sportsmen, many of whom would think nothing of effecting a quick change to this fact. And they very nearly had their way in the spring of 1993— a very dry May had left the bush tinder dry and susceptible to wildfires.

Two men drove their ATVs south from Elk Lake, forty-eight kilometres (thirty miles) to a freshly brushed-out trail that led to McGiffen Lake, deep within the wilderness park interior, and only two miles from the Lady Evelyn River. The Cabin—*my cabin*—was sixteen kilometres (ten miles) downstream. A seasonal northwest wind, typical for the month of May, was blowing briskly; the cabin was also downwind. The two men had used this lake access before, even though it had been created illegally within the protected area. They had established a small campsite and fished the lake for trout. This time they weren't fishing. One of the men took a five-gallon jerry can of gas and poured its contents in a long line along the backside of the campsite, amongst the dry scrabble of highly flammable spruce deadfall. The two men started their ATVs knowing that once ignited, the bush would explode quickly into an uncontrollable blaze. And it did. By the time it was reported, the men had retreated to their local drinking establishment boasting of their deed.

————————————

The garter snake that was curled up under my back moved slightly. The sensation slunk into my dream world without invitation, feeling more like caressing fingers than a coiled snake; suddenly realizing what it was, I sat up and pushed the snake to the floor. It must have crawled through one of the cracks in the log wall beside the bed. The morning mist outside, above the falls, lay in heavier than normal sheets; even the inside of the cabin seemed inordinately foggy for some reason. I could also smell smoke. I checked the cookstove but it was cold. I walked outside, stood on the cold rock in my bare feet, and looked upriver. Visibility was restricted to about two hundred feet, just to the apex of the upper rapids. The smoke smell was stronger, heavier, a pungent fragrance of burning spruce. Yesterday's wind had subsided and the air was still, thick but motionless.

"Get up, we've got to paddle up to Divide Lake!" I barked at Melissa as I threw on my pants. "Someone's left a campfire burning, for sure…smell the smoke, it's thick everywhere," half mumbling as I laced up my boots. We grabbed a rake, a shovel and an old "pisspack"—a five-gallon tank with attached backpack straps and a spray hose that I had liberated from the forestry department during my stint as ranger. It took us less than half an hour to portage and line the canoe up the rapids into Divide Lake, but by then the air had cleared and a fresh breeze out of the northwest began to pick up energy. We paddled to the narrows and climbed a high bluff to get a better look. It was obviously more than just a simple camper fire left by sloppy canoeists; this was an all-out, raging wildfire.

A flume of billowing grey-black smoke mushroomed skyward upriver from where we stood, maybe three kilometres away. The sound of water-bombers picking up water, probably on McPherson Lake, accelerating, taking off, filled the air with a nervous, low hum. "Let's get closer," I said, and we headed up the lake towards the fire. We passed three canoes moving quickly downstream. "Get outta here, now. The fire's moving this way, quickly," yelled one of the paddlers. They were gone before I could question them about any of the details. We walked the long portage around Shangri-La Falls, getting as close to the conflagration as we could dare. Helicopters buzzed noisily like hornets circling a disrupted nest. "We better go," I told Melissa. She was crying. "The trees, those beautiful pine trees…I can't believe this is happening," she lamented, gripping my arm, tugging gently. I had no response to give her; it was hard enough to hold back my own tears. One of the most pristine and vibrant sections of the river was up in flames. *A camper fire? A lightning strike?* Neither sounded plausible—few campers went downriver this early, and if they did, it would be a higher calibre paddler who would respect the law of the trail by keeping campfires well under surveillance; no thunderstorm had coursed through the district either; that left only one other cause—*spring fishermen.* With the gate open to the park until late June, anglers often camped at the river, plying the waters for trout, sometimes descending the river to the first set of rapids. But the camping area at the river crossing was well cleared and campfires were not likely to get out of hand. I was perplexed.

We paddled back to the cabin. The burnt aroma still prevailed and a blue haze settled over the falls and up through the pine flanking the valley. We had no radio, or any way to communicate to at least find out if we were safe to stay put. I didn't want to leave the cabin, and if I had to, I would stay and fight the fire as it approached—I didn't want to lose this cabin too. But I was responsible for my friends' safety; Melissa wanted to stay but I agreed only to hold back for one more day to see how events unfolded. Up on the lake, the wind was constant, pushing the fire closer to the cabin; at the falls it was sheltered from the breeze, allowing the smoke drift to settle. After a while, the pungent scent became abrasive, uncomfortable to take deep inhales, and if you did, each breath would end in a coughing spasm.

We woke up the next morning to a smoke-filled cabin. It was so thick outside that we couldn't see across the river, less than fifty yards away. "We have to leave," I told Melissa, reluctantly, and she knew that things had gotten worse overnight. There was no other choice. The route out would be a tough, sixty-five-kilometre (forty-mile) paddle to the nearest road at Mowat Landing, where we could get a ride to Temagami with a friend who would pick us up. For the first kilometre or so we would be paddling into the oncoming fire, upstream to Divide Lake where we would branch off and down the north channel, then away from the blaze. As expected, the smoke formed a grey wall at Divide, obliterating any recognizable rock or tree, and we found the exit portage by listening for the sound of the rapids to guide us. Once heading away from the fire we began to relax into a rhythm, moving steadily eastward, downriver past Helen and Center Falls, reaching Frank Falls and the Lady Evelyn Lake system by mid-morning.

The expanse of the lake afforded a panoramic view of the wildfire smoke plume rising ominously above Chee-bay-jing Mountain. It remained windy, adding to the intensity of the fire during the day, and I wondered how far away from the cabin it was, or whether the fire crews and water bombers even cared. The canoeists hightailing it down Divide Lake were told over a bullhorn from a hovering helicopter, to clear out. The fire was still about five kilometres (three miles) away from the cabin. The only thing slowing its southeasterly progression towards the cabin, was the landscape patterns; Dry Lake ridge rose five hundred vertical feet, running north and south, acting as a natural barrier, but if the fire ranged north along McPherson Lake, it could follow a low bank of spruce-filled muskeg and easily circumvent the ridge.

Melissa and I hitched a ride into Temagami from Mowat Landing, tired, anxious, and thoroughly dehydrated and hungry. In our hurry to vacate the cabin, we had taken little with us for the long paddle out. Barry Dawson, the town postal clerk and avid fly-fisherman, saw us walking down Main Street. Bursting out of the post office door, he caught up to us.

"They're trying to burn you out!" he announced. "Who's trying to burn us out?" I replied, remembering that Dawson was well connected to the district gossip grid. He kept his ear to the ground, and although he sided toward the melodramatic, most of his information was reputable. He fancied himself as an environmental crusader, of sorts, keeping our little band of eco-warriors up on the latest town scuttlebutt. He had not honed a good relationship with the town folk, but being a large man and ex-RCMP detective, nobody would entertain the thought of challenging him to a bar brawl—and nobody wanted their mail tampered with.

"Elk Lakers—two of them—they were boasting about it in the local bar last night and someone overheard them," Dawson explained, saying nothing more and returning to the post office. *Shit. So, they actually did it, the bastards. They burned out the park, just like they said they would.*

I had to wait until the next morning to visit the forestry office. There was a caffeine buzz to the place, everyone running around, coffee cups in hand, pant legs tucked into government-issue boots. The acting supervisor was reluctant to talk to me, at least about the *real* cause of the fire, maintaining that it was filed as a "recreational class fire," and that they had no such suspicions about the fire being purposely set by Elk Lakers. The fire was now under control; fire crews—numbering over one hundred and fifty men—back-burned a line of forest, taking advantage of an abrupt change in the wind direction. The blaze had extinguished itself by burning itself out; in all, over twenty-five square kilometres (about ten square miles) of pine forest had been razed, terminating at the narrows on McPherson Lake. But it had been a "hot" ground fire, hot enough to cause boulders to explode and leave the landscape scorched and barren. The government man refused my request for an investigation, but assured me that he would personally "look into the matter" concerning the illegal access road in the park. Neither would he reclassify the fire to something other than a "recreational" fire—*that* pissed me off. It now looked as if careless canoeists rather than crazed pyromaniacs driving ATVs set the fire.

Melissa and I returned to the cabin, driving the three hours around the north end of the park and camped at the gate where the road crossed the Lady Evelyn River. Fire crews were still in the area, dousing spot fires and maintaining a minimal presence in case it flared up again. The portages had been destroyed, the campsites the victims of incendiarism and the rapids too dangerous to run in the canoe because of the fallen, charred trees. The tops of some of the downed trees were still foliated but burned out at the roots, causing them to collapse into the river. We climbed the high ridge above McPherson Lake to assess the damage. It was one of my favourite "listening" places, where one could look back over the royal legions of pine, and retrace the route along the river, with a full view of the chutes we had just portaged around, rested, perhaps thrown a line in to catch some trout for dinner.

It was all gone. The eminent quartz monolith that sat proudly at the apogee of the hill had been blasted apart by the intense heat of the fire; gnarled, wind-sculpted pine that had taken centuries to root amongst the scrabble of rock, proud and tenacious, struggling against the unremitting cruelty of the elements, lay in a charred heap like blackened pick-up sticks, their roots no longer touching the earth they had so enduringly embraced. There was no soil left, nothing, just charcoal remains and blackened granite for as far as we could see.

Melissa was crying. And that set free my own emotions that I tried so stoically to veil under a varnish of disbelief and silence. It was hard to remain proud and valiant in the face of such wanton destruction. We cried with and for the earth that day, at least for that slice of wilderness rubbed raw to the bone by the chafe of ignorance. Standing, overlooking a wasted land, clutching each other, there were no words of consolation to share. Descending the ridge, footsteps exploding in powdery ash, we were impatient to move on, and we paddled the rest of the way to the cabin without speaking more than a few words.

If there was any consolation to the fire, an epiphany of some greater consciousness or cosmic revelation, it was the immunity of the cabin. Safe beyond the ravages of unrequited anger, anchored to the shadow of a rock shield, it was impervious to the machinations of the outside world, existing within its own sacred space. Affixed to that disclosure, was a realization that my own persona was ensconced within the physical and spiritual existence of the cabin. I was safe here as well, untouchable, free of mainstream woes and perils. To live here, though, was a fanciful escapist's taunt—I knew that—but I could at least find sanctuary here when I most needed to rejuvenate my soul.

Fire is the most unpredictable of all the forces of Nature; its character demonstrates a firm control over all living things. It creates its own energy, its own hot breath—consuming and terrible but somehow divine and scintillating. Fire destroys, but it also resurrects and revitalizes a forest as part of the cyclical genesis of Life. Metaphorically, the Lady Evelyn fire presented itself as an illumination of my own spirit that direly lusted some kind of restructuring. In exchange for man's inhumanity towards Nature, I wanted to rebel against man; and man was uncurtained behind vicious rhetoric and exploitation.

I wanted to make a visible stand, to assert my territory—to send a message back to those imperious bureaucrats and heartless brush apes that I was a force to be reckoned with. I was still not vindicated for the loss of the Wapaho cabin, and now *they* were trying to take away Cabin Falls, by whatever means possible. I needed to build another cabin.

Fourteen: King of Sladen Township

Or like the snow falls in the river,
A moment white—then melts for ever...
Robert Burns—*Tam O'Shanter,* 1790

In the wake of the 1980s environmental tsunami, when people actually cared about the health of the planet, came a wave of self-indulgence. People were tired of feeling guilty about deforestation, global warming and world poverty. North American consciousness turned inward, focusing on social malaise like job security, health care and lifestyle stability. Mainstream environmentalists compromised away wilderness to maintain a credible, agreeable composure amongst the industrial elite. Shaky partnerships were consolidated between greens and browns because the green movement was starving, proving that money *can* buy ecological propriety. Key earth warriors, tired of paltry salaries, were often absorbed into the ranks of corporations, and turned against the crumbling grassroots stronghold. Jobs versus the environment—a moral and ethical dilemma, a dilemma which slowed the environmental movement in Canada to a mere crawl.

The prospect of building another cabin at the falls was not an impulsive decision; it was all about timing. When I had met the owner, Richard Lathrop, two decades earlier, I had asked if I could construct my own cabin on the property. The request was launched several years before I became a third-part owner. Lathrop obliged without question; he had admired my tenacity and passion as an environmental activist and the work that I had done to protect the river. He also knew that without my intervention, the cabin would have been expropriated; it was also in a sad state of disrepair. The old cabin was showing its age, and it was constant work trying to maintain its humble appearance with just paint and roofing tar. The addition had been built some time ago; still, I had the yearning to build something entirely of my own design.

I had begun to guide commercial trips to the cabin, for executive retreats, a couple of times a year, mostly to raise the profile of the property so that it would be more difficult for the government to think about expropriation. But the cabin was tiny—too small to house eight men, two stoves and a working kitchen. If I were to maintain the cabin as my home for a good part of the year, and to operate it as a tourist business, I needed to expand the living area. And the very notion of building anything at all, at a place that many would consider paradise (including me), involved a huge ethical consideration.

Since 1980, the original cabin had not been locked, kept open for passersby in need of shelter. I had also begun a "Tripper's Journal" where paddlers could leave a diary entry, a poem or sketch of their adventure. I had received a letter from an American, and a cheque for thirty dollars to cover the costs of the few items he had used while staying in the cabin during an early spring trip. He was travelling with his ten-year-old son; the weather had turned foul and the young boy developed pneumonia. Both were hypothermic when they accidentally stumbled upon the cabin. Finding the door open, they quickly made a fire to warm themselves. The father told me that his boy would surely have perished if it were not for the open cabin. They stayed several days until the boy was strong enough to paddle out. I had often come across paddlers using the cabin for shelter; this was sometimes a nuisance when I wanted to enjoy my own sanctuary, but I was still embarrassed about "ownership" of such a fine retreat in the middle of a publicly owned wilderness park. People were starting to refer to me as the "King of Sladen Township"—certainly the only taxpayer in the district. Being "king" had none of the titular qualities for me; the original owner, R.B. Newcomb, honorary "King of Temagami," went berserk and chopped his wife up with an axe. Having my own cabin, set apart from that tidbit of tainted "history," would guarantee my private space while staying true to original values—to offer sanctuary to anyone who needed it.

Level building sites were non-existent—the bedrock dropped or tilted off in all directions, forming broken tiers along the edge of the falls. But that made it even more challenging. A new cabin also had to be inconspicuous—an obligatory prerequisite to placate the possible consternation of old-school paddlers who would critique such an undertaking. I could utilize on-site cedar for foundation posts and beams, and cut only enough spruce off the property to supplement what else was needed for additional beam work and floor joists.

I chose a building site about thirty metres (one hundred feet) below the Rapidan cabin, facing the pitch-off to the falls. A rock buttress would support one end of the cabin, while the opposite end would be raised almost three metres (about ten feet) off the ground, giving the new cabin a "tree house" feel to it. Few cedars had to be removed, and those that remained would shield the new cabin from view. It was perfect.

My friend Melissa and I had returned to the cabin after the fire. Metaphorically, it was like getting back on the horse again once it bucked you off. It felt as if the government sponsored the fire in a subversive way and I needed to show them that I was here for the long run. We got to work immediately, even while government helicopters were still flying over, extricating fire crews. Several good-sized spruce trees were cut down behind the property, the bark was peeled off easily with the spring sap still in the wood, and the lot was piled out in the sun to dry out.

The helicopter returned over the next three days, hovering annoyingly over the cabin, and I could see someone taking pictures through the side window—*five times in one day!*

I had to put a stop to this harassment. When the chopper returned, as usual, approaching the cabin just above the treetops, I grabbed my rifle (it was unloaded) and climbed on to the roof in full view. I pointed the gun at the helicopter as it flew over. It veered away suddenly and never came back again. Several days later, after we had completed building the foundation for the new cabin, we were back in the town of Temagami talking to my friend Doug who worked at the Forestry office. He knew about the incident with the helicopter, and that it had raised quite a stir with the authorities. It wasn't just the antic with the firearm, Doug informed us, it was the cutting of trees in a wilderness park. An observer on the helicopter reported my cut logs.

"We didn't cut trees in the park!" I retorted, not holding back my anger. "It was on my own property, damn it!" Doug told us that they were about to send in a conservation officer and a cop with the intent to charge me, but Doug intervened and explained to the officials that the property was technically outside the park, and that I owned the timber rights to the two acres along the west side of the falls. To say that the local authorities in the forestry office were miffed would be an understatement. Doug had saved his superiors from the embarrassment of laying false charges. If the property were on a government lease or land-use permit, like most cabins constructed on Crown Land in the province of Ontario, I could have been charged and fined. Whatever deal was struck between R.B. Newcomb and the Premier of Ontario back in the 1930s, to actually secure a *deeded* lot on a waterfall, must have been a blood pact between best of friends.

As the 1990s yawned into the era of narcissism, I enjoyed my own period of hedonistic pleasures and self-indulgence. In an attempt to cut free some of my partisan ideals and jaundiced opinions, I managed to work conjointly with the Manitoba government and Parks Canada, to produce a wilderness-canoeing guide to the wild rivers of Manitoba. It was a dawning of a new age of environmentalism, for me—an awakening to the realities of the movement away from the mainstream into an independent, purely Machiavellian methodology—that the *ways justifies the means.* Battles may be fought and lost in the boardrooms, but wars could be won in other, less compliant ways. It was all about the *process.* It was like building forts when we were kids: you could throw together whatever you could find, and build something without tools or effort, and watch it get blown down by the first wind storm; or you could put some thought into the *process*—start with a solid foundation and use hammer and nails to construct something of substance and strength.

I had learned from my good friend, Bob Hunter—co-founder of Greenpeace—that working "from the inside" (in his case, through the media) worked far more effectively than trying to wage war as a paid lobbyist. He was absolutely right. I knew that I had made an effect in Temagami by producing the canoe guidebook with the intent of promoting a non-consumptive use of resources. The Manitoba book would be my fifth project, and to snag a prey as huge as a provincial government was a magnanimous coup for me. Like Ontario, Manitoba was rife with environmental and cultural atrocities, against the land, and against its Native Peoples. I managed to secure the sponsorship of the government to explore nineteen wild rivers—most of which were threatened by logging, mining or hydropower development. It was a grandiose challenge that would take me four years to accomplish. Aside from rubbing noses with fate, in the guise of polar bears, wildfires and deadly rapids, I also met Stephanie.

Four years had gone by since I had started building the new cabin; the foundation had been built using simple tools and the art of wood butchery—no power tools and no level. Organic carpentry. I was caught up in my own busy life, travelling by canoe far from my home paradise, living sporadically with women I had no right to, exercising my own brand of self-indulgence. With Stephanie, it was different somehow. I had to be accountable; not just for my actions, but for my emotions. It wouldn't be easy—there would be constant maintenance to keep the flame alive—but the fire would sizzle and burn like sulphur on a tin plate.

We lived different lives, two thousand miles apart, but it was the wilderness that brought us together. Embarking on one of my Manitoba adventures, she and her husband came along as clients. He was an aspiring young dentist with a new practice in Nelson, British Columbia—Stephanie was an artist. It soon became apparent that this was not an enduring relationship. Stephanie had fallen in love with the guide. The marriage ended, but not precipitated by any act of impropriety by the guide—I maintained a rather steadfast, almost puritanical personal rule *not* to get involved with a client. What transpired between trips was entirely a different matter.

Dubious of Stephanie's motives for giving up a financially secure lifestyle to traipse around with a wilderness guide, I exposed her to several contrived "tests" that might assuage my trepidations. "Can you open a tin can with a hunting knife?" I asked. She stabbed the top of the can with her knife and aptly sliced open the lid to reveal the contents. "Can you piss out of a canoe?" I knew I had her on this one. Even Tom Thompson, famous Canadian painter and supposedly adept canoeman, may have met his fate this way. But instead of standing up and arching her bottom precariously over the gunwale, she simply peed in the empty bailing can and safely dumped the contents overboard. I was impressed.

One of the true tests of our relationship unfolded as a rather awkward drama during a late October canoe trip into the Temagami interior—two days away from the cabin. We had only been together for a few weeks. Camped by the side of a small river system, basking in the late fall sunshine, we procrastinated about returning to the cabin even though ice had begun to form in the quiet pools. By sunrise the next morning, the river had completely iced over, too thick to break through, but not strong enough to hold our weight.

It was a tenuous hike along the irregular shoreline, tugging at the loaded canoe like an irresponsive dog over the ice. Fallen timber impeded progress and tempers flared quickly as we tired of the heavy work. We seemed to make little progress for our labour. Stephanie would cry every so often and I wasn't as sympathetic as I should have been, my annoyance at her emotional outbreaks only drew more tears. At one point, the canoe became wedged on a log, tight enough so that we both had to strain hard to extricate it, and when it did release, it happened suddenly, sending us both sprawling into the Labrador Tea sedge on the riverbank, rolling in laughter. After several hours, we eventually reached Florence Lake and the headwaters of the Lady Evelyn River—still more than a long day paddle from the sanctity of the cabin. We were greeted by a vicious headwind out of the north that dropped the temperature to well below freezing. It was dark by the time we reached a suitable camping site. It started to snow. Ice formed quickly along the Lady Evelyn shorelines, leaving only a thin line of open, black water that, by morning, might also be frozen over. Wet, cold, hungry, with still a hard paddle to the warmth of the cabin, we ate quickly by the campfire and retired to the warmth of our nest. The feel of our skin together under the blankets assuaged the angst of our situation. Too tired to even think about making love, we lay content listening to the ice-flakes slide down the sides of the tent, musing about the day, slipping slowly into blissful sleep as the cold stillness enveloped the waiting world around us.

There was just enough open water to allow the canoe to pass through easily; in places where the ice formed a complete barrier, we were able to push the canoe through without difficulty. The black water of the river, what remained of it, contrasted sharply with the white of the encroaching ice sheath. Our stilled world resembled an Ansel Adams or Curtis photograph—stark, almost surreal, lifeless, save for one tiny canoe whose occupants pressed the limit of their welcome, past the time when even the loons had migrated to their Louisiana wintering grounds, and when all manner and forms of wildlife who endure the long, Canadian winters, seemed to be in stasis, waiting.

For the two of us, there was an excitement in the danger of being isolated and vulnerable. It also defined the strength of our relationship and the ease with which we could work together under duress. The usual traits that embody a work-in-progress relationship, the idiosyncratic personality quirks, like toilet seats and toothpaste in the sink, weren't in the same genre as crashing your canoe through river ice. Yet, I saw in my partner a naïveté to the present dangers that I continually made light of. Through my own experiences, I knew well that a simple miscalculated paddle stroke could mean an upset in the rapids and a quick death in the icy depths. I had been there before and had since counted my blessings. I had respect for cold water. Stephanie had unconditional trust in me. It seemed as if anything were possible.

Life in the wilds, although romantically pinioned within the framework of fantasies depicted in adventure novels, has its share of hard realities. Romance wears thin in blackfly season, and sangfroid calm dissipates rapidly with a black bear trying to rearrange your pack. And money—there's never enough to pay the bills. But Stephanie persevered. Sitting by the stove that hyperborean fall, thawing out body parts and smoking cheap cigars, we had made plans to finish building the new cabin.

The following spring we arrived at the cabin soon after break-up. Lumber had been purchased and piled on the dock at the airways in Temagami, to be flown in to Divide Lake, upstream of the cabin. Each stick of wood, nail and sheet of steel roofing would have to be moved a total of nine times before it reached the building site at Cabin Falls. But as we sat there drinking our morning brew, looking out over a dreary, spring landscape, waiting for the rain to stop, we knew that each board would be that much heavier to carry over the portages. For two weeks it rained and snowed, and the stack of lumber sat forlornly at the airways absorbing moisture. We had no phone. At the mercy of the weather and the prognosis of the float plane pilot, we waited to hear the drone of the engine overhead. When it finally arrived, we bolted for the canoe to meet the plane. Much to our dismay, the lumber mill had delivered the wood and stacked it on the dock in reverse order, which was fine if we were to start building the roof. It was another week before we could lay the floor and build the walls of the cabin. Content with transporting building materials, we had moved over four tons of supplies to the site. Working in the cool mornings, before the onslaught of biting flies, we would carry about thirty loads over the trails, or raft the lumber in one-half ton loads down the rapids from the lake, moving whatever the plane had dropped off, closer to the falls.

By mid-June we had framed in the cabin. Exhausted but elated about the amount of work we had accomplished, we had to leave to finish the Manitoba book project of mapping wild rivers. After paddling nearly three thousand two hundred kilometres (about two thousand miles) that summer, we returned to Lady Evelyn River in late September to finish putting the roof on the new cabin. Before the snow descended in the waning days of October, the new cabin had been closed in but certainly not finished. There was still much work to do, and at least as many trips over the portages carrying lumber and supplies as had been brought in already. But we could leave it for the winter, knowing that the respite from the heavy labour would last for six months while our bruises, blisters and backs had time enough to recuperate. By December there was something else to consider—Stephanie was pregnant.

Fifteen: Paradise Below Zero

---

*Come quickly spring! Come and lift us
to our ends, to blossom, to bring us to our
summer, we who are winter-weary
in the winter of the world.*
D.H. Lawrence, 1885-1930

The Beaver pilot levelled the plane off at a thousand feet. By now the droning of the engine had worked its way into the pit of my stomach, wrapping the ball of butterflies into a knot of worries that I hoped Stephanie wouldn't read on my face. I wiped the beads of sweat off my forehead, turned to the back of the cabin where Steph sat with the kids, and made some comment about the drabness of the landscape below.

"The fall colours are all over with," I yelled, competing with the howl of the 1950s DeHavilland Rotax engine. Steph nodded but said nothing. Christopher was perched on her lap, breastfeeding, almost asleep, while Alexa, almost four months old, was asleep in the basket car-carrier, sitting on the vacant passenger seat. The back of the plane was packed with boxes of provisions, snowshoes, skis, packs filled with winter clothes and cartons of books and art materials. The other half of the load remained behind and would be brought in tomorrow with our friends from the TV station.

Did I remember everything? I couldn't stop going over the lists in my head, repeating them constantly until everything congealed into one vague lump which made things infinitely worse because now I knew for sure that something we needed was missing. I'd worry about it later. Right now I had to concentrate on being stoic and self-assured; Steph was watching me carefully, and if I were to crumble into a swirling vortex of emotional soup and let the croutons of sensibility sink into oblivion, she would lose it for sure. I wanted to vomit. I was both excited about what lay ahead, but full of angst about such an undertaking with such young children, and a wife who had never even winter camped before. Six months was a long time. And then I began worrying whether or not we were doing the right thing at all. The adventure was quickly becoming mired by doubts, and the doubts began to cloud my vision of Paradise as a *journey*—it now seemed as if we were running from our failures.

I could read the lakes below like a topographical map unfolding; having paddled those waters many times over the past three decades they were indelibly etched in my head. And as the sun reflected back off those dark blotches like the steady flash of a camera I became mesmerized until a sense of calm replaced the nausea. I started to doze off just as we were passing over the highest point of land in Ontario—Ishpatina Ridge—and according to Ojibwa mythology, this was the place where Nenebec had turned the mountain into a snake, and where world transformation—flood to rebirth as a great terrestrial island—had played out a scenario not unlike the Christianized story of Noah's Ark. Ishpatina's deep canyons showed as huge scars across the snakes back, brazened by abrupt cliffs and tumbled scree, never explored, perhaps never to be explored. The more I thought of it, the more I wanted to go there, just to set foot on a tract of earth where no other human foot had tread; to visit the place where the world began, at least the world according to local legend, and that was as close to *the beginning* for me. The trip would be difficult and without any other purpose save for some silly obsession I had, and I knew that when I arrived there, standing amongst the rock scrabble and green alder, looking up at the sheer granite walls, I would see the ancient writing that would explain the Great Mystery. Suddenly I wanted to be alone. Life would be so simple—like it was before.

I took a quick look behind me. My babies were sleeping; and in that repose of innocent calm I regained my own sensibility of purpose. My own fatigue prompted an irrational and almost melancholic depression, and it slipped silently and insidiously into my consciousness at times like these, during brief moments when I had nothing to do except interview my own perverse thoughts. I knew too that my alter ego was there to remind me of my filial duties. Shame.

I fell asleep, nodding and jerking with the dips and surges of the Beaver manoeuvring through the airfoils. The pilot was querying about the landing site below in a thin voice when the plane banked sharply. I could feel Steph's fingers dig into the back of my shoulder; the veil of sleep that had taken me away to some netherworld was lifted. I reached around so that she could hold my hand and she took it and squeezed tight enough to induce a wince of pain, and she didn't let go until the Beaver had landed and was taxiing up to the shore of Divide Lake. My neck hurt, my hand had been compressed in a vice and my stomach had been ravaged by nervous tension. "Great flight," I said to Stephanie, "feels good to be here, finally, doesn't it?" Stephanie complied with a deep sigh. Christopher unlatched and Alexa began to cry.

Soon there was a mountain of boxes, packs and assorted packages strewn across the bedrock landing. We pushed the Beaver off the shore, telling the pilot that we would meet him here tomorrow when he brought in the rest of our gear. Five minutes later, after the plane had cleared the high ridge behind us, the only sounds were those of the wind in the white pine and a crying baby. Steph took Alexa out of the bassinette and breastfed her; moments later, Christopher latched on and became drugged with warm milk, all the while watching as I moved boxes from the landing to the two canoes tethered along the shore.

The second canoe was towed along, jerking with every paddle stroke, straining against the weight, and once we reached the rapids, while Steph carried the babies along the portage (one in a front carrier, the other in a back pack-frame), I nursed both canoes through the maze of rocks, trying not to get hung up. This time of year there was more rock than water; hard to believe that it was getting that difficult to get one canoe down through the channels when in the springtime we would raft two canoes, side by each, loaded with a ton of supplies, and have no problem finding room between the boulders.

We left most of the boxes at the head of the next portage and took only what we would need for the night across the trail, along with one canoe, and headed for the cabin. We all needed some sleep and I had little motivation left to start slugging heavy boxes over the portage so late in the day. The kids were getting as cranky as their parents, and by the time we arrived at the cabin landing, they were both wailing in full unison, enough to put Steph and me at odds with each other too through the sheer tension of the moment, induced by a rather tenuous day of road, air and canoe travel.

Inside the cabin it was cool and dank which added to the displeasure of two hungry and diaper-soaked infants. Fifteen minutes later, the fire in the cook-stove had dispersed the chill, dinner was baking in the oven, the kids had been changed and Mom and Dad were sharing a scotch. Life was good. Life would be great once we had all the supplies across the portages and we could finally settle in to our winter nest. There was so much to do in the next few weeks, but we would worry about that tomorrow. The kids were sleeping, the gentle rhythm of the falls working its charm as a watery lullaby. The fire crackled in the stove and we elected not to turn on any lights other than a single candle lest the abruptness of artificial light purge the softness of the evening ambience. Just to sit still and do nothing, to think of nothing, was blissful.

The next two days were deliberately busy, meeting the plane and the arrival of our two friends from the TV station, moving gear and equipment downriver to the cabin and attending to immediate chores. Bob Hunter—ecologist specialist and co-founder of Greenpeace, was covering our story for CITY-TV out of Toronto. Stephen Hurlbut, news director and cameraman, was producing the show to kick off our website journal, aptly called "Paradise Below Zero," which we were to feed three times a week to the station news website. Transmission would be made by way of a satellite phone and laptop computer, supplied by the station and bolstered by an extra solar panel to help power the battery bank. CITY also gave us a digital camera to use so that we could send visuals of our adventure over the Internet.

This all sounded uncomplicated, but in fact it added to our compounding list of things to get done over the diminishing time before winter set in. To begin with, I wasn't a keen advocate of the cyber-world, nor was I adept at figuring out how any of this stuff actually worked. I was still perplexed as to how a simple AM radio transmitted music and voices over the "air." As a writer I was a dismal failure at attending to current whims of the editors I worked with who insisted I "get on line" and send copy by e-mail. I was still married to my typewriters, one being a vintage Underwood finger-banger that found an honoured place here at the cabin. I loved the sound of the bell as the carriage slipped past the right-hand column indicator, and the requirement to be a part of the mechanism of writing. It was a physical, as well as a cerebral exercise, whereas the monotony of staring into the electro-magnetic face of a computer screen, for me, was tantamount to personal demoralization with venomous aftereffects. Cyber-friends of mine had succumbed to a variety of computer-induced ills, from miasmal nervous tension, repetitive strain syndrome to deteriorating eyesight. The worst that could happen to me on my trusty Underwood is a couple of blistered fingers, or accidentally knocking my coffee over when returning the carriage. Now, I looked in horror as we unpacked an assemblage of high-tech gadgets and widgets that would be left up to me to figure out. The technicians at CITY gave me a twenty minute run-down on equipment set-up, plugging wires here, shifting antennas there, this goes in to this, and don't do this or you'll delete your file, *and whatever you do, make sure this is attached like this or you'll fry the circuit!* Information overload. Nothing sunk in. They must have realized they were dealing with a computer dimwit so they wrote out all the instructions in long hand for me to take with me. As it turned out, it was all the wrong information.

We enjoyed spending time with our friends; we wouldn't see them for at least six months, but we were also glad to see them go. They got their video footage and sound bites. Now I was free to get my work done. I stood on the rock landing and waved goodbye to my compatriots, not moving until the Beaver cleared Dry Lake Ridge to the west and I could hear nothing but my own breathing, and the smell of avgas was replaced with the scent of sweet fern, balsam and dry pine needles that clustered in the crevices of the granite. I sat for a moment, lit my pipe and let the spiced aroma drift lazily around my head. Feeling that I should take this moment to reflect, relax and indulge in the aloneness, I mused about the choice we had made and the fact that there was no turning back. Soon there would be no float planes flying as the lakes and rivers iced over, and there was no place for a helicopter to land safely near the cabin. I was hoping that Stephanie was feeling the same about our adventure as I was. There were issues. And I knew they would erupt at some time or another. She was more gregarious than I was; I just hoped that I would be good enough company for her not to get restless or bored. I hoped that I could muster enough patience and understanding too—traits that were seriously stretched out of whack by the tedium of the past few months.

I wanted to take my time on the return paddle to the cabin, mostly because I knew that I would get few moments like these again, and that I would have to work harder than I had ever had to work before. Staying south to help pack up our things lost precious cabin-prep time, but Steph needed the help and support, and I resigned to the immutable truths that the work ahead, during the storms of November, would be more than hostile. The important thing was that *we were all here.* Although tired before the task even began, I felt strong and ambitious and looked forward to the coming winter with unabashed enthusiasm. I prayed for at least two weeks of good weather first, though, so I could collect enough firewood to last us until the river ice set strong enough to hold our weight. As long as I could paddle freely on the river, I could easily cut firewood and get it moved close to the cabin. But as I dipped my paddle in the blackwater, and watched as drips bounced across the surface as ice pellets, I knew that freeze-up was imminent.

There was bated expectation of a November rife with sunny days and snowless skies; surely the gods would be kind to us, be sympathetic of our impromptu situation. False hopes. Nature holds no favourites. And as humans have designed their fate with peculiar regularity in the face of the coming storm, we were to be undistinguished and alone with our precarious state of affairs. The verity of having no firewood and a cabin that could barely keep itself warm, let alone a family of four, compounded the anxiety of our arrival in Paradise. There would have to be compromises. And compromises often exacted a high price. And in situations like these, the male and female minds seem to work at different levels of consciousness, especially when there are small children and creature comforts in the equation. The cabin demanded attention, but without firewood, that haven would quickly turn in to an icebox. Regardless of the chores that presented themselves, or at what level of priority, the babies needed constant maintenance. Diapers had to be washed at least twice a week, and that was a major project in itself requiring the mucking out of the diaper pail where soiled diapers had been brewing for at least two days; then there was the hauling and heating of water for the hand washer, dumping the sludge away from the river; the rinse cycle where everything had to be done again; and then figuring out a place to hang the wet diapers where they would dry within a few hours in order to keep up with the demand. And it rained often; that meant rigging up a drying system in the cabin near the stove instead of expecting the cold drizzly days of November to dry clothes outside. Apart from the steady need of clean diapers, Christopher was mobile and inquisitive. That presented a problem of making sure everything was childproof and safe—not such an easy task when the cabin was perched at the lip of a thirty-foot waterfall.

There were several places along our decks and footpaths that fringed the river where the current was strong enough to carry off a two-year-old in a matter of a few seconds should he stumble off the invisible barrier of safety. The deck off the main cabin had been fenced with chicken wire but there was a myriad of other spots where the footing was precarious, where we had to grasp his hand whenever we ventured beyond the front deck. But a two-year-old can dart like a hummingbird and has no sense of danger. Alexa was content in the back-carrier or playpen, but Christopher seemed to move in ever-increasing distances from the main cabin and wailed if we tried to leave him alone even for a few moments while running to the outhouse. One of us always had to be with the kids. And that presented their own set of problems when it came to how much time either of us would spend with them.

I needed to get the basic chores accomplished, soon, but that meant that Stephanie had to be with the kids most of the time—and that was an unresolved issue. More and more, Steph needed time and space away from family to gather personal energy lost through the birthing process. That meant that I would have to spend a good portion of my own time tending to the kids and leaving the chores until some other time, which normally I wouldn't have had a problem with. And, Stephanie wanted desperately to feel as if she were helping, outside of the realm of motherhood, to cut wood, to bang nails, to carry lumber over the portages, anything. I argued that, time dictated a somewhat deliberate and experienced hand at attacking the list of chores, and although her desire to help was endearing and noted, her time now was more valuable and practical as a mother, and that would allow me the margin of time I needed to ready our winter nest. After a heated discussion we came to an agreement about our itinerary—that I would be free to do the necessary jobs so long as I was there to help with the laundry, and to watch the kids for an hour each morning, and whenever I wasn't occupied at work away from the cabin. Stephanie would attend to the immediate chores of organizing the cabin, but mostly it stationed her as a babysitter and milkmaid while I had the freedom to work outside. This, I assured her, was temporary, just until the major tasks had been undertaken.

And then there was the computer stuff to figure out. It all sat in boxes and cases upstairs in the loft, waiting, taunting, lurking. The satellite phone was hooked up and working. That was easy. I had built a shelf below the gable window where the phone could be perched for clear reception and transmission. I was proud about that little accomplishment. It was setting up the laptop that remained a daunting task, and I left it for several days while I attended to more important things. Although we were expected to file journal stories and photographs upon our arrival, I managed to stall the programming by creating a façade of problems that didn't yet exist. The computer gadgetry was safe while they sat solemnly in their related cartons. I would deal with it later.

The job of cutting wood to feed a stove would seem to be a rather prosaic undertaking, which may prove to be true of any place other than Paradise. Paradise did come with its own brand of classical tasks, most of which required mathematical configuration, not to mention the Herculean efforts to enact and accomplish them with any efficiency. Menial chores required a certain amount of vision, stalwart stamina and the precision of a covert military operation. Like the rocks in rapids, trees seem to move on their own volition in accordance to some otherworldly purpose; a straight tree that stands dead

and ready for cutting, suddenly leans one way, opposite to what you want, and that could pose a variety of problems and dangers unbeknownst to the neophyte sawyer. Not only does there need to be an overall battle plan, each manoeuvre needs to be calculated according to the tenets of good woodsmanship, and more importantly—gravity.

I could cut deadwood either up or downriver from the cabin—nearly a kilometre for each stretch—high-grading only the deceased, standing spruce or pine, colloquially known as "chicots." Specie selection was important; first of all, there were no hardwood trees and that meant cutting only the softwoods (pine and spruce), which were lacking in energy output on a comparative basis with hardwoods. Softwoods also left few hot coals so that meant that the stoves would have to be fuelled constantly. Spruce burned better than red or white pine, which was fine since I was reluctant to cut pine anyway as they were often used for nesting by a variety of animals and birds. And there was a surfeit of spruce along the river, both standing and wind-felled.

Topographically though, there was a resident hindrance that reared up like the shield of thorn bushes in the tale of Snow White, replete with dragons protecting the bounty. The shoreline was either boulder-infested, or swampy, and once you got beyond the initial veneer of rocks and scrabble and muck, there was a tangle of dense cedar, snags of fallen black spruce, hidden grottoes and foot traps, slippery side-slopes and steep inclines. Once you found a chicot, you also had to plan the actual cutting of it and how it would be moved downslope to the shore.

Over the years that I had used the cabin, firewood was gathered rather spontaneously, taking what would be needed for the relatively short duration of the stay. Now I had to plan a major incursion into the forest for at least six months worth of firewood. I still had use of the canoe; I could transport wood a long distance and move it to within a few metres of the cabin. There still needed to be a plan because I wouldn't have the luxury of easy travel for very long. I also had to think of how and where I would get firewood once the river froze over. Our immediate needs required enough wood to last through the freeze, when travel was restricted to the vicinity of the cabin. I estimated that freeze-up would last about six weeks.

I opted to cut wood as far away from the cabin as I could paddle the canoe, and as far upslope as I could walk. This would leave the available wood required later, when I had to deal with deep snow, closer to the shore and cabin. It was a good plan—it was just near impossible to consummate without undue hardship. Upon our arrival at the cabin it had rained almost constantly for a week; then it turned cold, forming a slick patina of ice over everything—rocks, logs, canoe, paddle—everything was slippery. Still, it could get worse—*it could snow!*

At this time of year, just before freeze-over, there occurs a rather peculiar phenomenon, familiar to those who have dipped their paddles late in the season. The water becomes "thick," like oil, gelid, heavy, and whether or not it remains to be just an illusory eccentricity of Nature, I have yet to determine. Paddle strokes that once sliced the water like a warm knife through butter, now plowed and laboured sluggishly, ice forming up the shaft as far as one's grip. Rather than gliding effortlessly, the canoe hesitated after each surge. The change was almost invisible, but certainly enough for me to notice. Having spent most of my life in the canoe, I could easily detect any deviation in how the canoe reacted in the water.

On several previous occasions I had pushed the envelope on fall weather, staying well beyond the fringe of time between open water and ice-over, enjoying the dog-days of late October—when temperatures hovered above the freezing point in the day and the sun would trick you into a complacent lethargy. But days had been deceivingly short, and the long nights of below freezing temperatures worked quickly to transform water into black jelly. Getting out of bed to see a frozen river panorama is a rude wake-up call to the reality of how quickly the change can happen. The ice is seldom strong enough to carry your weight; thick enough at times to impede any attempt at canoeing through and breaking the ice like an icebreaker. The only resolve is to walk along the shore hauling the canoe and gear by rope over the ice.

After a week of solid rain, I was finally able to get out to cut firewood. Although anything worth cutting was thoroughly soaked, the water levels rose high enough so that I could now run and line the canoe (loaded with firewood) down the rapids above the falls. Even the standing chicots were wet and frozen and this made the job rather tenuous. The wood was heavy to move and I knew it wouldn't burn well; it also weighed the canoe down so that the gunnels were dangerously low to the icy water. Running the rapids with a canoe loaded with firewood, normally, was not a problem—I had done it many times before. Now, however, there were other factors that exacerbated a conventional chore. A layer of ice had formed over most of the river rocks, either from spray or rain; wherever I needed to get a solid footfall there was nothing but neck-breaking slickness. I was working alone too, and I had to configure the safety of any of my actions. A broken leg was one thing, but even with a life jacket on, I could fall, knock myself out and slip into the black water face down. I had heard of it happening before. That, in itself, added to the tension of moving firewood from A to B. I could manipulate the sluggish canoe down the first part of the cabin rapids, the current assisting in the manoeuvres, but halfway down the channel took a quick dogleg over a ledge that was not passable without me having to get out and physically push the boat through. The moment I stepped out of the canoe my legs wanted to go in separate directions. I would slide over the boulders on my ass trying to get a solid perch, all the while wrestling with a frozen rope tied to a seventeen-foot stallion that weighed half a ton. The final drop plunged a metre through a crevice just wide enough for the canoe; the resulting momentum vaulted the boat dangerously towards the lip of the falls. At this point I would have to force the canoe over to a quiet eddy that lay directly below the cabin—not an easy task considering the now heavy flow over the falls. By the time I managed to get the load to the safety of the shore I was a nervous wreck, and I would stand for several minutes supporting myself against a cedar tree before unloading, knees clacking together like a metronome.

For the amount of effort, not to mention risk, the pile of firewood grew ever so slowly. From the minute we lit the first fire in the cookstove, the home fires would burn continuously for the duration of our six-month stay in Paradise. Initially, with the uninsulated ceilings staring down at us like the inside of a whale's rib cage, the old cookstove could hardly keep the cabin temperature at a comfortable level. *And it wasn't even that cold yet!* Firewood seemed to disappear into the hungry maw of that stove faster than I could collect it. Sweaters and fleeces were donned as soon as we got up in the morning; Alexa's playpen was pushed close to the side of the stove so that she could benefit from the radiant heat while Christopher, always on the move, began his vigil of circling the stove in inquisitive and bold exploits, burning his fingers enough to eventually learn *not* to get too close.

Temperatures continued to drop towards mid-November and there was still no respite from the constant freezing drizzle. Eventually, I had to abandon trying to float the firewood down the rapids by canoe. Not only did it become too icy, but the flow had increased to a dangerous level and the risk of an upset too great. I knew my own limits. The scenario of being washed over the falls, pummelled by the firewood I had just cut, played over in my head like a B-movie. My only resolve was to cut as much firewood as I could and stack the unsawed bolts at the head of the portage leading to the cabin. That was the best I could do under the circumstances. I could then cut and split firewood as we needed it and, it was hoped, there would be enough stockpiled to see us through the impending freeze-over.

There was precious little firewood available anywhere near the cabin; the closest deadwood, up or downriver, was left intact and standing for later use when I had to collect it by snowshoe. The amount of firewood we needed was totally speculative since I had no idea yet as to how quickly two (and sometimes three) stoves would consume softwood spruce. When I was homesteading in the Laurentians I had the good fortune to have access to maple, beech and yellow birch—all hardwood species that yielded long-lasting coals and high heat output. I could load up the stoves in the cabin in the morning and not worry about them for hours. I knew exactly how much wood to cut and how quickly it would burn in each stove.

The charge of procuring firewood during the rains of November, although a tenuous and dangerous task, would later be considered a frictionless occupation. Once the snows of December settled over the tumbled, ancient landscape, there would be new hazards to contend with. But for the time being, as the felled deadwood pile created a small mountain at the end of the cabin portage trail, there seemed to be a sense of security in knowing that, for a short time at least, the home fires would remain stoked and I could now attend to other pressing tasks.

When it finally stopped raining, it simply began to change to snow. Heavy, sodden snow, thick like hardening plaster, adhering to any and all exposed surfaces, save for the circle of ground beneath the canopies of the largest pines. Native Canadians once celebrated the arrival of the first snow with feasting and merriment. For us there was little exaltation. As the world around us turned monochromatic in a solemn beauty, it only seemed to accentuate our unpreparedness. Any work outside would become more laborious, and as it turned progressively colder, the open black water of the river added a residual dampness to the frigid air.

With the firewood chore temporarily out of the way, the next occupation was to move indoors and attend to the immediacy of winter-prepping the cabin. Since it was constructed on a steep decline, the underbelly of our sanctuary lay exposed to the cold winds that coursed downriver from the north; not only were we losing heat out of the roof, but the floor remained chilled enough that we refrained from removing our mukluks while inside the cabin. The ceiling came first. Fortunately, with the help of two friends, we had moved the bales of insulation from the landing site over to the falls during a short visit to the cabin earlier in the year, shortly after Alexa was born. The pile of bales practically filled the entire space of the old log cabin. We had only to move them over a short catwalk and deck that led to the new cabin—a relatively easy job once the snow had been shovelled off.

It felt good to be working indoors; it was the first time in two weeks that my hands were warm. Steph and I worked diligently for two days straight, insulating the entire ceiling, stapling up plastic vapour barrier to close it off, halting work only for diaper changes, quick meals and fire-stoking. The cabin now had its hat on; the heat once lost through the roof now loitered lazily within the confines of our winter abode. Even the cookstove seemed to rejoice by not having to work so hard to pump out the heat. Using sheets of heavy black plastic-wrap, the underside of the cabin was closed off, effectively deflecting the ever-increasing intensity of the late November winds. Inside the cabin, sweaters were shed and the babies played comfortably at floor level for the first time. The average inside temperature rose to a pleasant 70 degrees Fahrenheit and we hadn't even fired up the second stove. But that would come soon enough as the temperatures dropped steadily as December neared.

Following two days of above freezing temperatures, the remaining veneer of snow was enough to signature the movement of birds and animals that ventured near the cabin: white-footed mice (by the droves), a red squirrel, raven, weasel, and even the rompish river otter, made unseen visits to Paradise. During the daytime, while we were bustling about, the forest seemed devoid of all life forms; the traces of activity by forest denizens assured us that we were not alone.

After nearly three weeks in Paradise we took a break from the tedium of work and treated ourselves to the first family outing. Sporting winter garb, freshly pulled from storage bags, we paddled downriver to Twin Sisters Falls—one of Lady Evelyn's grandest of cataracts with a vertical plunge of nearly twenty-five metres (eight-two feet). From our vantage point at the precipice overlooking the canyon above the falls, we stood in awe of what lay below. Creating a menagerie of bizarre sculptures, the drifting spray off the falls had performed magic upon the bleachers of rock and gnarled spruce, coating everything with a thick membrane of ice. The trees were in frozen stasis, bent under the weight as in supplication to the deity residing over the falls, veiled white and motionless, silenced and immobilized by winter's breath.

From our perch above—a levelled platform of rock still unfrozen and unsheathed in snow or ice, pine-needled and warmed generously by the sun that now broke free of its shroud of cumulus—we sat quietly. Childless, Steph and I would have stayed indefinitely, bundled together, perhaps even made love, but the dictates of parenthood and the soft cries of a baby molded every waking hour. The cold would work its way through the bundle of fleece and wool, a diaper would have to be changed, Christopher would become restless and it would be time to move on. It would be a slow walk back to the canoe, well-knowing that this would be the final paddle until break-up next spring, nearly half a year away. Staring into the black water as we paddled along I tried not to think of how dangerous it would be if we tipped the canoe. It was like staring into the dark recess of a room you were not allowed to enter, knowing that something lurked, waiting, watching your every move; an upset would be disastrous, even this close to the cabin.

Snow, and lots of it, about thirty-five centimetres (fourteen inches), accumulated while the wind chill pressed the temperature to minus twenty-five. Paradise was closing in around us. For me, the isolation administered an introspective objective, or rather a reality check, a rationale for being here, and I grasped for any reason, cosmic or otherwise, for dragging my wife and two babies into the dark veld of deep winter in the wilderness. I sat under the snowy pines, ruminating on that very thought. My life, *our lives,* back in the mainstream had become suffused with the drone of everyday annoyances: the discord of driving on streets where road rage was accepted as typical social exchange; needless trips into town; invasive telephone solicitations; bills—the profligate consumer madness; marching it seemed, to some other drumbeat other than our own. The act of leaving our truck parked in a snowbank for six months somehow seemed rebellious, psychologically and emotionally uplifting. A cleansing, I suppose, in New Age terms.

I prefer not to address my time spent in the wilderness in terms of "survival," although at times it certainly felt as though Stephanie and I struggled with the vagaries of such harsh conditions. And those conditions may have bordered on the outer rim of personal adventure. Adventure, in itself, denotes a particular fascination with risk taking that is beyond the comforts of our normal, daily wanderings. The term "survival," before being bastardized by Hollywood flicks, conjures up a particular situation that may take place in either an urban and wilderness theatre, presenting profound and absolute danger under extreme environmental or confrontational conditions without an immediate guarantee of rescue. North Americans seem to hold a peculiar and almost perverse and pornographic attachment to *real* drama that embodies the fundamentals of survival, relishing in the plight of others, masking it under the guise of "news," keeping informed, when it actually presents itself as a macabre form of entertainment.

Wilderness survival, for us, materialized as a struggle to maintain a loving relationship and a belief system that was constantly under criticism from those in the mainstream. Having already acquired the necessary skills to attend to all our basic, primal needs, it was just a matter of exercising those proficiencies as required by immediate and long-term needs. The onus for "survival" was on me since Stephanie was more or less a winter debutante. The challenge was readily accepted and the tasks selflessly indulged with a stalwart eagerness. There was no struggle to survive the onslaught of a cruel winter, but rather a casual embrace of winter in terms of "living" within an environment to which we had become accustomed and much preferred. But, as with any wilderness adventure, success is gauged only partly by *what* skills can be drawn upon; the greater will of "survival" having a more intangible presence as inner strength and psychological astuteness. In our case the task of living comfortably simply demanded physical labour and not a lot of deep thought. What lay at risk was our love for each other, the very survival of which depended upon how each of us reacted to the stresses of parenthood under somewhat peculiar conditions. What vaulted this family adventure from the mundane to the profound was the addition of two babies into the survival equation. Others had done this before but without children. I did it thirty years ago, spending the better part of a winter with a university friend, not far from our cabin on the falls. The adventure unfolded with simplistic verve. And now, three decades later, with a young wife who had never been winter camping, ever, and with two babies still at her breast, the "journey" seemed almost incredulous and utterly selfish on my part. I wanted to experience the transition from fall to winter, and from winter to fall, two vacant accreditations to my service as wilderness adventurer. I was here, finally, come hell or high water, two babies or not; I pushed the boundaries hoping the bubble wouldn't burst. But, instead of feeling closer to Stephanie I seemed to be drifting off in my own world. Concerned more about my lack of current accomplishments than the sanctity of family, banking somewhat on the protracted success of the adventure before it unfolded, I expected my wife to simply join in on the program I had designed for us all. It wasn't working. And as I watched my beloved wilderness freeze over, the very nature of the process became symbolic in our relationship. There were ice walls building up between us; the flow of loving conversation stopped as if frozen by such great expectations that defined us as lovers, parents and best of friends. The assault of responsibilities, the heavy work at hand, the lack of money, the retreat into the wilderness, left us at odds with each other. Instead of bringing us together, Paradise was driving us apart, insidiously and efficiently, with the sharpness of an ice crystal on cold steel. And there *was* no sunshine, just dark, long nights and blustery, cold days, dirty diapers and endless chores. But there was also a beauty around us that beguiled the senses; an austere magic that played about the surroundings like mischievous elves, painting and sculpting a work of art on the face of Nature. And without that wonderment, that enveloping sense of awe, Stephanie and I would have nothing else to share. Through the layers of ice the light still penetrated and I knew in my heart that there was still hope for us.

Today the batteries went dead. Our connection with the outside world was terminated. The satellite phone and computer gadgetry drained our bank of dry cells. The low trajectory of the sun, obscured for most part by the tops of the cedars surrounding the cabin and by the ceaseless mass of storm clouds, made the solar panels seem purposeless. We simply drained what power there was in each of the twelve dry-cell batteries. We now had to break out the gas lanterns for light. There was precious little gas for the lights and the nights in Paradise started at four o'clock in the afternoon. I had somewhat mastered the computer set up, or rather configured the machinations of cyberworld into my way of doing things. It wasn't pretty but it worked, and the TV station was receiving our transmissions—until now. I had placed a distress call to the station just before the batteries went dead, exclaiming that we should have had a backup generator to charge the bank of batteries when required. The station told us they would try and get the air service to fly a generator out to us. Divide Lake was still free of ice, but the river had almost totally crusted over. Filing stories on time was less of a concern than the ability to keep connected with friends and family. For Steph it was a lifeline; she could still, somehow, feel closer to her friends at a time when she needed them, even if only through the occasional phone call or e-mail. For me, it was an emergency line in case something happened and one of the kids needed to be evacuated. I still couldn't get my head wrapped around the idea of having any such contraption that may taint the otherwise perfectly "wilderness" ambience. At least there was the satisfaction of not being able to *receive* calls.

Stephanie wrote letters to all her friends and family—long letters. But when the sky thickened and snow began to fall, we both knew there would be no plane coming in and no mail going out. Then the tears came. To Stephanie the winter now seemed interminably long. Sitting at the table, fiddling with her package of aborted mail, the weight of our situation fell heavily in long sobs. Instead of comforting her I got angry. "What's wrong with my company?" I blurted. Before she could answer we heard the *thwap-thwap-thwap* of a helicopter above the cabin. We ran outside on to the deck in time to see the chopper drop below the falls, hover about three metres (about 10 feet) above the frozen bog near the shore, while someone started heaving boxes out of the cargo door. "Quick, the mail!" Stephanie yelled, shoving the package into my hands. My boots were already on, and without putting on my parka I ran down the steep, icy ledges of the lower portage to the canoe landing at the base of the falls. By the time I had the canoe turned over, the helicopter abruptly left the scene. I waved frantically but to no avail. It was gone, probably in a rush to avoid the ever-worsening weather.

I had to break ice to reach the floating bog mat to retrieve the boxes that were slowly sinking into oblivion. There was a small gas generator, a box of miscellaneous hardware, and five five-gallon gas jugs half sunk in the muskeg. I pushed the canoe up onto the beaver grass and stepped out on the frozen, but unstable ground, piled the booty into the canoe and paddled back to the landing. It took three trips to get it all up to the cabin. I refrained from going inside because I knew Steph would not be happy about the mail not getting out. At least now we could get the phone system back in operation. "Call your friends tonight," I suggested later, hoping that would console her enough to forget about the letters. "It's not the same," she replied, "letters are more intimate, personal…I can't say what I want on the phone."

"That's all we have right now, the phone, it'll have to do," I reminded her without much feeling. I just wanted to tell her to get her act together. *That* was a sympathetic response. The river continued to freeze over.

Yesterday I took the canoe out for a final paddle, restricted to the quickly receding half-circle of open water below the falls. The natural, white foam caused by the aeration of water-borne organic matter, usually seen as ghostly wisps of soap-like tentacles trailing out from beyond the black pools below rapids and waterfalls, had now retracted to mere frozen discs resembling communal wafers, bumping and clacking impatiently against the rampart of growing ice in a musical protest.

Had it not been for the snow-covered ice along the shore I would not have known that a large wolf had wandered to within five metres (sixteen feet) of our spring near the foot of the falls. The tracks were well defined, probably three days old, made when the snow was wet, now lightly dusted with fresh powder. The wolf had stopped within fifty metres (fifty-eight yards) of the cabin, and probably sensing our whereabouts, he had turned and climbed the steep slopes to disappear amongst the big pines. It made me wonder as to what we may have been doing at the time of its visit. Sleeping? Chopping firewood? Baking bread?

Firewood was getting low by the end of November. One morning, just before dawn, I walked by snowshoe to the upper river and looked north from the portage. Using a stout pole I tested the ice along the shore by giving it a hard whack. Not even the slightest crack. About two inches of ice, I figured—strong enough to sustain the weight of a team of horses (so I've been told). Towards the middle of the river there were still large voids of deadly black water surging between the neoplastic hummocks of snow. It wasn't safe enough to travel on yet. Deep sighs. Maybe tomorrow.

Light snow falling. Solemn and sombre, the almost constant gloomy days of November have come and gone, leaving us with only scant memory of fall. The wonder of transition from the verdant autumnal landscape to the monochromatic brilliance of winter, in no small way, has tempered a sort of ecstasy in our minds, as lone spectators witnessing some divine, elemental phenomenon. We view each changing winter scene from our safe bubble, relaxing into routine, assimilating to our newfound lifestyle in the wilderness. Still, sadly, I feel a separation from this beautiful family, resentment, a closeness borne of motherhood and the connection children have with their mother that I don't have, fathers don't have. We all sleep in the same bed, the babies melting into their mother's breasts, feeding, falling asleep; I sleep on the edge of the bed so that I don't wake anyone when I get up in the morning. Our relationship was running somewhere between lukewarm and cold.

I try to spend time with my son. It's a lot of work just to get him dressed for the cold. Outside we never let him stray; it's far too dangerous to let him wander on his own. I hold his hand a lot. His inquisitive nature slows my pace to his. It's quality time and he teaches me more about life than I could ever have imagined. Everything is new again through his eyes, and in that sparkle of innocent curiosity I search for the right answers. It's all about changes—adaptation. The world around me was changing—not just the landscape, but my *whole life*. Steph was right—*nothing would ever be the same again*. Stephanie would never be the same again. I was charging along at high speed, just as I'd always done before and I'd fight so hard *not* to conform to some ordered plan.

Why was change so hard to accept? My own two-year-old was wiser than I. He knew. Somehow he was trying to communicate that message. But I was too stubborn to listen, clinging to some fleeting essence of a past life. My freedom was threatened.

But as the winter progressed, the days became less toilsome. The perplexity of isolation, the interminably long nights, the uncertain precipitation, unstable ice conditions, dissipated as if winter had finally found its quiescent rhythm. And with that change evolved complacency within the walls of the cabin, our own rhythm finding harmony with the lifestyle we had chosen and with each other. By January we were travelling over the river ice without difficulty or danger, except once when Stephanie fell through while skirting a wet spot on one of the packed trails. Her skis broke through the punky crust and she went down into the cold water up to her waist. Alexa was on Stephanie's back in the carrier, oblivious to the danger; I was ahead with Christopher riding in the pulk. By the time I had realized something was wrong, Stephanie had pulled herself out. It was an event that highlighted the resident personality of the river in winter—that although the world above the frozen surface of the river appeared steadfast, there was still a restlessness beneath us.

For something in my life, our lives, that had epitomized serenity and freedom, the cabin had unexpectedly become a prison to us. Our world had been drawn in tighter and tighter as the tasks of daily life—pioneer life—compounded into drudgery. November and December had proffered little sunshine to brighten our days, and without even a weekly ration of halcyon cheerfulness, those days became arduously laborious. As the sun rose higher in the winter sky, and the crispness of the blue sky suddenly broke the tenebrous pall of lightlessness, our moods danced with newfound hope. The adventure continued. We stopped marking off the days on the calendar.

A pine marten began making frequent visits to the feeding station positioned two metres (six feet) from the kitchen window, where Christopher would perch himself and watch with fascination as this strange, cat-like creature devoured bacon rinds. By the end of February, there were four martens vying for the few table scraps we could afford to donate to the feeder. And they would scrap and carouse noisily under the cabin where they had fashioned their living quarters. With the appearance of the pine martens, there was a dramatic decrease in the number of mice in the cabin.

March Equinox was a remarkable "turning point" in this winter journey; the balance of day and night, dark and light, emphasized the cosmic duality of our relationship as an organic family—that life would unfold in regular phases, in and out of darkness, eventually finding balance and harmony. It wouldn't be easy. But then, nothing in my life had been easy—and I seemed to thrive on unremitting challenges.

As the snow melted away in the cordial days of April, we were once again compelled to live within the close shell of the cabin; the once smooth winter trails now collapsed into the natural folds of the land, and the river swelled and pulsed with new and dangerous vitality. The last of the ice flushed over the falls in a great celebration of freedom. Although I had intermittently felt shackled by cabin life, there was an immense release of pent up tensions and doubts between Stephanie and myself. Whether or not we actually accomplished what we set out to do was an abstract enigma with no plausible answer aside from the fact that we made it through the six months alive. There were emotional bruises, healed partly by the sheer beauty of the changing landscape, and as partners sharing a remarkable journey with two precious babies who were still too young to remember any of this.

Robert Newcomb, the "King of Temagami" and the inaugural prince of the Land of Shadows, built a cabin on the shore of the Lady Evelyn River in 1930. He had failed to live at peace in this wilderness, stricken by the relentless crush of responsibility, and he enjoyed the sanctuary of the cabin for only a short inhale of his life. I, on the other hand, inhaled deeply of this wild elixir and let the aroma embalm my soul.

"But you love Temagami more than you love me," lamented Stephanie. How could I answer that remark without compromising one or the other; *was it possible to love a physical place more than a person?* Can a person divulge a sense of security, or afford sanctuary from the ceaseless drone of civilization? The cabin, perched on the precipice of the trout stream, offered unconditional acceptance of my love, a love for the wilderness that defined us both.

Afterword

I went to the woods because
I wished to live deliberately,
to front only the essential
facts of life, and see if
I could not learn what it
had to teach, and not,
when it came to die,
discover that I had not lived.
Henry David Thoreau— *Walden*, 1854

Of memory, Oscar Wilde would ascribe to a more poetic justification, that our own history is simply the "diary that we all carry around with us." Carl Jung, of course, would label it as the "baggage" that defines our failures. For me, the search for sanctuary is no longer an ephemeral mystery, but a consciousness gauged by a tolerance for the mundane. Sanctuary—like the Great Mystery—surrounds us at all times—*semper eadem*—attainable only should we *not* become overburdened with our own shortcomings, depressed by our own baggage and, at some point along the trail, learn to shed some of the weight.

The Cabin, over the past few years, appears not so much as a physical place of sanctuary, but a final, esoteric, personal challenge of the eternal fitness of "order." My life has embraced the ideological acceptance that *chaos eventually leads to order;* if I am ever to assimilate to that order, however structured, there must be a purging of the old order and an accepting of change as a positive entity not as an assault on my soul.

The new cabin is not yet complete, nor is my evolution to that new order of existence. It took over 60 Beaver aircraft loads of lumber—36,000 pounds in all—to construct what I believed to be a salvation from the relentless pressures of life. Hand carrying eighteen tons of physical material into Paradise to build a cabin, was simply a self-fulfilling exercise in hard labour—nothing more. Granted, the cabin is lovely, and provides a welcome roof for my family, but it has also been physically and financially draining. I have since realized that sanctuary is not a tangible possession, but a state of mind and heart. Like love. My love for the wilderness adheres to old philosophies entrenched in an inexplicable battle against authority; the battle still rages, but with a refined passion and a higher level of tolerance. My children taught me a new sense of liberalism of heart; my wife, very frustratingly, taught me to accept human love as a condition of acceptance—that nothing, not even the simple and unrestrained life on the wilderness trail can supplant the power of human emotion.

Photo of Hap Wilson, courtesy of Stephanie Aykroyd.

About the Author

Hap Wilson has been a wilderness adventurer and guide for over 30 years. A self-taught writer, artist and photographer, he is also one of Canada's best-known canoeists and the author of several books, including *Canoeing, Kayaking and Hiking Temagami, Rivers of the Upper Ottawa Valley: Myth, Magic and Adventure, Missinaibi: Journey to the Northern Sky: From Lake Superior to James Bay By Canoe, Wilderness Rivers of Manitoba: Journey By Canoe Through the Land Where the Spirit Lives* and *Canoeing and Hiking Wild Muskoka: An Eco-Adventure Guide.* His hand-drawn maps and illustrations were featured in *Voyages: Canada's Heritage Rivers,* which won the Natural Resources of America Award for Best Environmental Book. Wilson worked as actor Pierce Brosnan's personal skills trainer in the Attenborough movie "Grey Owl." He lives with his wife and two children in the Muskoka and Temagami lakes district of Ontario.

Hap Wilson's recent entry, "Follow Your Blissters," in the International Regional Magazine Association annual awards, as submitted by *Cottage Life,* won an Award of Merit in the General Feature category. The judges said: "Hap Wilson's achievement in building this cabin is matched by his writing—crisp and well-paced.... Gentle humour in the lead carries into the rest of the article, providing an engaging thread to tie together personal experience, observation and research."

Books by Hap Wilson

Hap Wilson is best known for his eco-tourism/travel guidebooks. *Temagami Canoe Routes,* his first book, was published in 1978 by the Ontario government and it soon became a Canadian best-seller; it is now in its tenth printing. Other books include:

Rivière Dumoine

Rivers of the Upper Ottawa Valley

Canoe Trip Log Book

Missinaibi: Journey to the Northern Sky

Wilderness Rivers of Manitoba

Wilderness Manitoba

Wild Muskoka

Voyages: Canada's Heritage Rivers
(winner of the 1994 Natural Resources Council of
America Award for "Best Environmental Book")

Hiking, Canoeing and Kayaking Wild Temagami

The Cabin: A Search for Personal Sanctuary